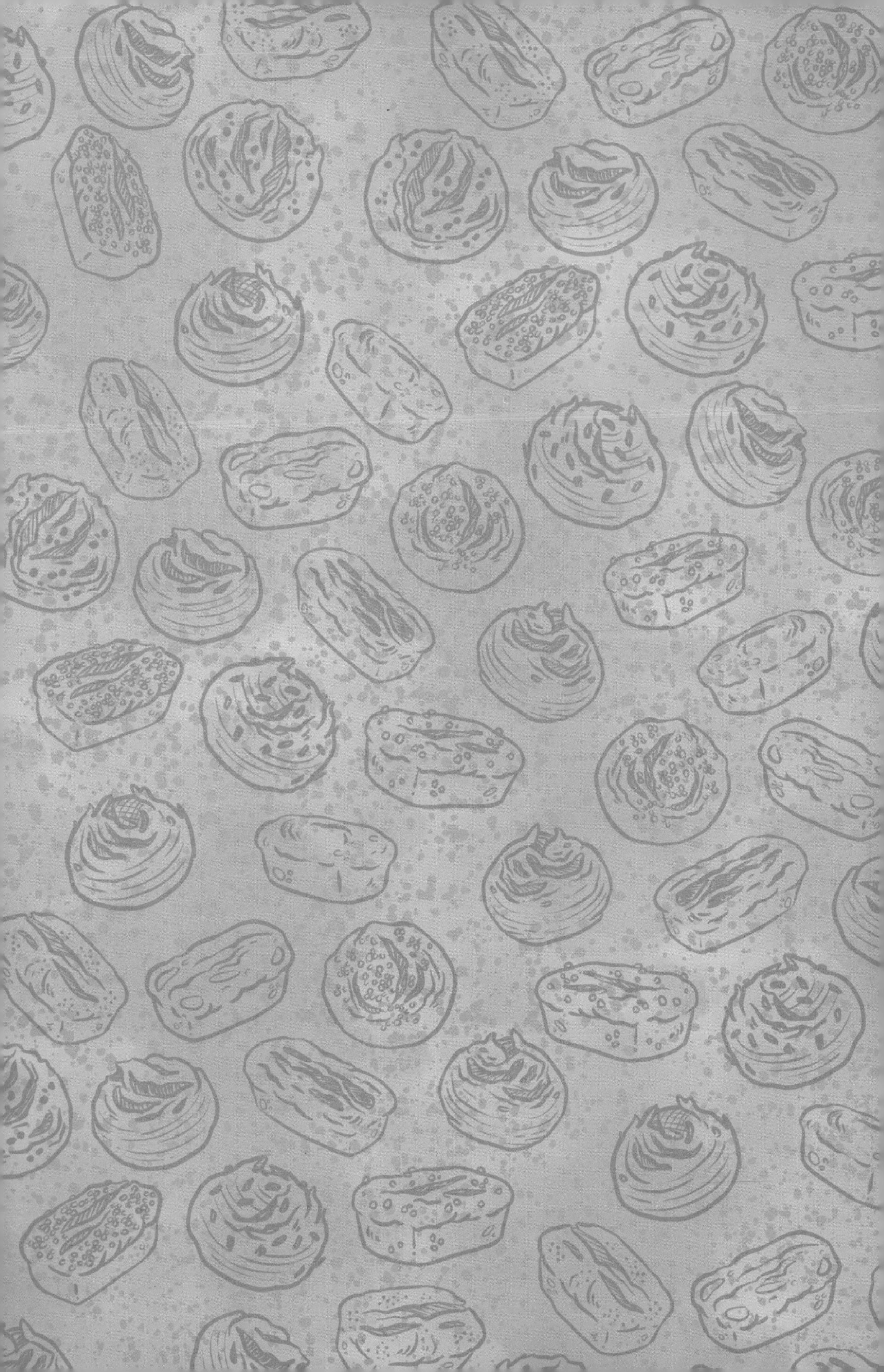

LET'S MAKE
BREAD!

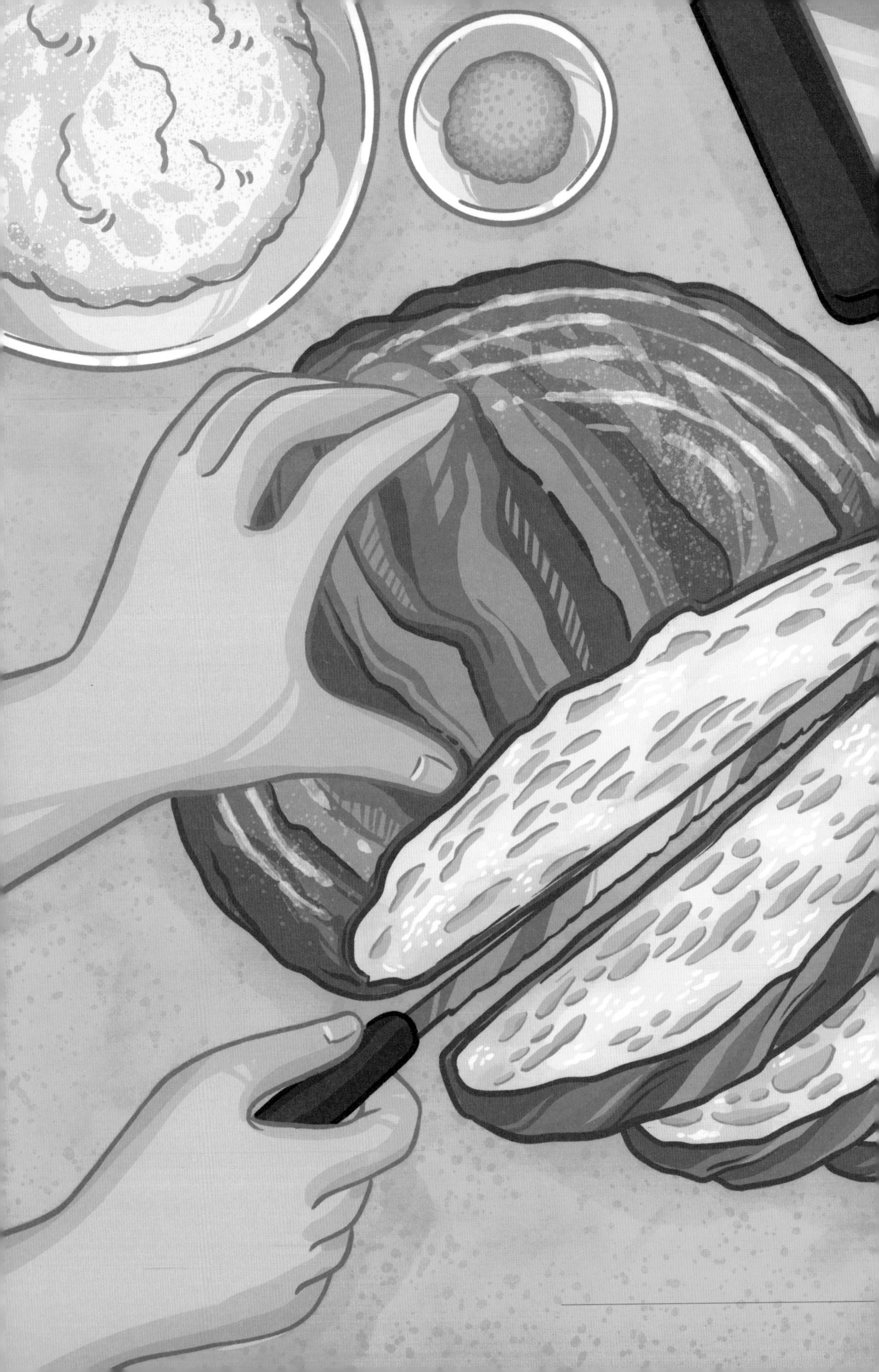

LET'S MAKE
BREAD!

KEN FORKISH

SARAH BECAN

A COMIC BOOK COOKBOOK

TEN SPEED GRAPHIC
An imprint of TEN SPEED PRESS
California | New York

TABLE OF

CONTENTS

THE FIRST RISE

HI. I'M KEN FORKISH, FOUNDER OF KEN'S ARTISAN BAKERY AND A JAMES BEARD AWARD–WINNING COOKBOOK AUTHOR.

AND I'M SARAH BECAN, A COMICS ARTIST AND ILLUSTRATOR.

AND WE'VE JOINED FORCES TO EXPLORE THE WORLD OF ARTISAN BREAD BAKING!

I OPENED MY FIRST BAKERY IN 2001 TO MAKE BREAD, CROISSANTS, BRIOCHES, AND MORE.

AND I'VE WRITTEN A FEW BOOKS ON HOW TO ADAPT THE TECHNIQUES WE USED FOR THE HOME KITCHEN.

FLOUR WATER SALT YEAST

THE ELEMENTS OF PIZZA

EVOLUTIONS IN BREAD

I LOVE COOKING, BUT I'VE ALWAYS FOUND BREAD BAKING TO BE INTIMIDATING.

ALL OF MY EARLY ATTEMPTS FELL FLAT, AND I THOUGHT I JUST WASN'T ANY GOOD AT MAKING BREAD.

BUT WITH A BIT OF PRACTICE AND SOME OF KEN'S SMART TECHNIQUES, I'M BAKING PRETTY GREAT LOAVES THESE DAYS!

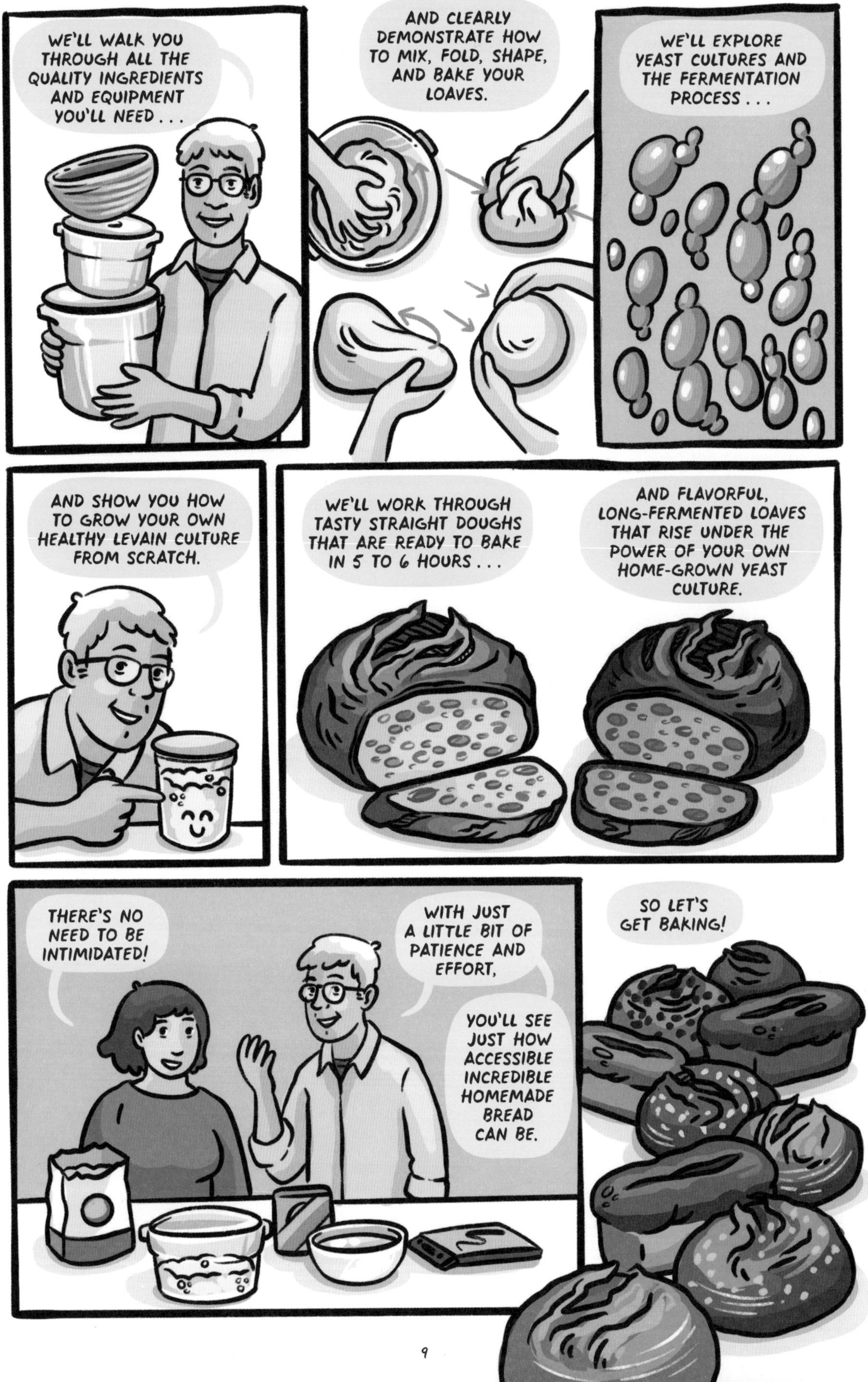
WE'LL WALK YOU THROUGH ALL THE QUALITY INGREDIENTS AND EQUIPMENT YOU'LL NEED . . .
AND CLEARLY DEMONSTRATE HOW TO MIX, FOLD, SHAPE, AND BAKE YOUR LOAVES.
WE'LL EXPLORE YEAST CULTURES AND THE FERMENTATION PROCESS . . .
AND SHOW YOU HOW TO GROW YOUR OWN HEALTHY LEVAIN CULTURE FROM SCRATCH.
WE'LL WORK THROUGH TASTY STRAIGHT DOUGHS THAT ARE READY TO BAKE IN 5 TO 6 HOURS . . .
AND FLAVORFUL, LONG-FERMENTED LOAVES THAT RISE UNDER THE POWER OF YOUR OWN HOME-GROWN YEAST CULTURE.
THERE'S NO NEED TO BE INTIMIDATED!
WITH JUST A LITTLE BIT OF PATIENCE AND EFFORT,
YOU'LL SEE JUST HOW ACCESSIBLE INCREDIBLE HOMEMADE BREAD CAN BE.
SO LET'S GET BAKING!

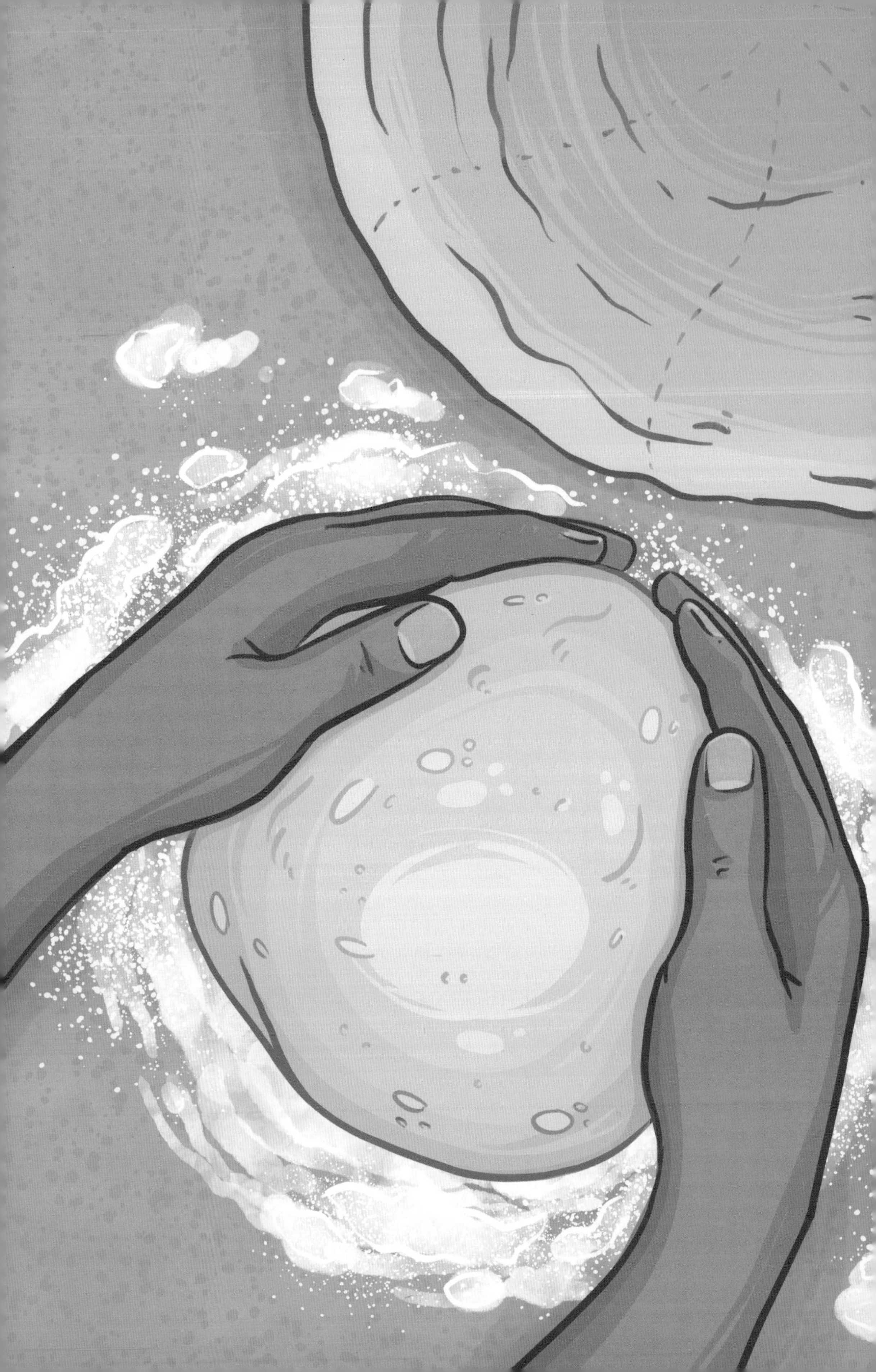

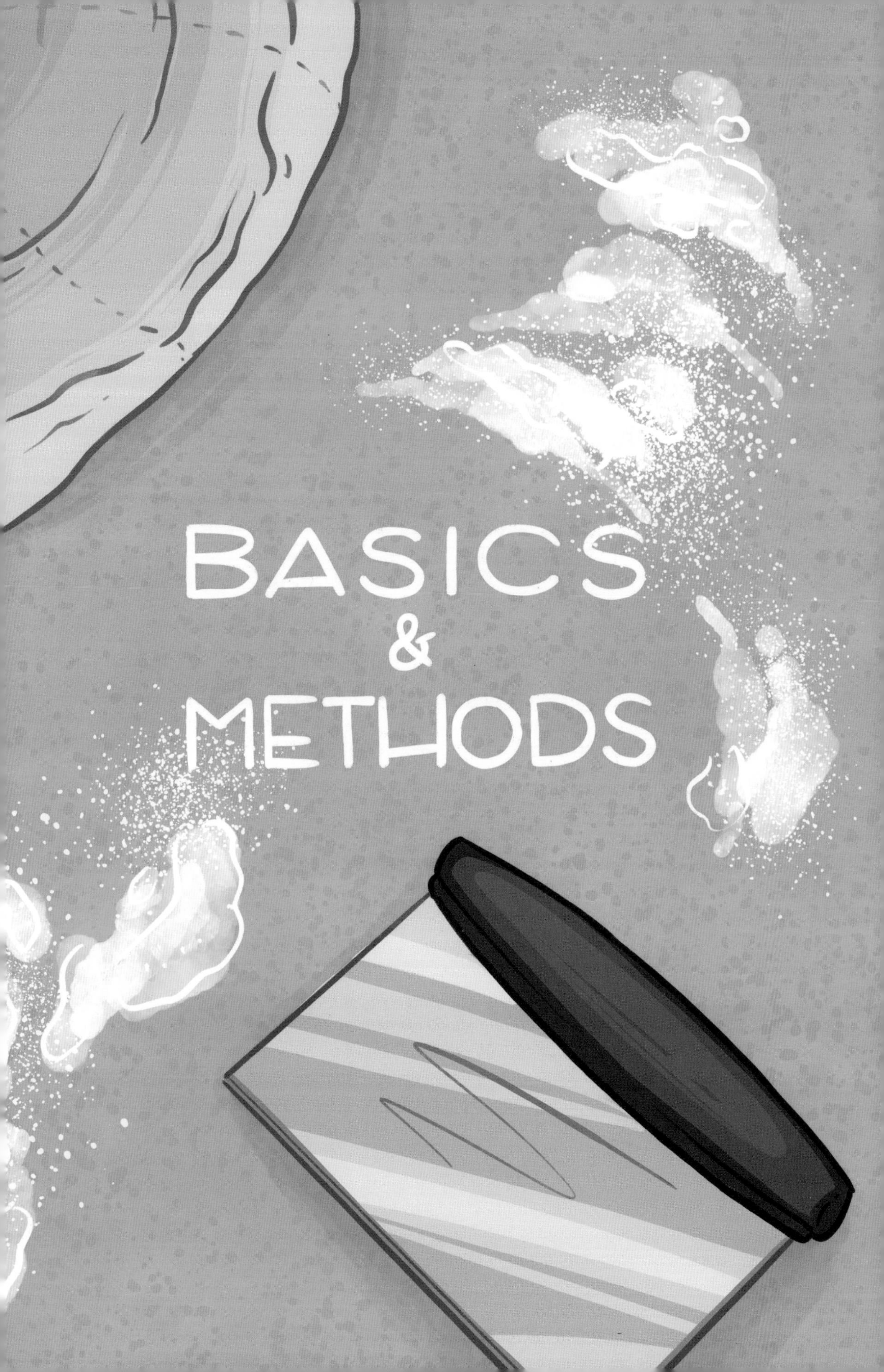
BASICS
&
METHODS

THE JOY OF BAKING

DECADES AGO, I DECIDED I WANTED TO BE A "MAKER"...

AND EMBARKED ON A QUEST FOR IMPROVEMENT THAT NEVER ENDS.

EVERY LOAF I BAKED MADE ME WANT TO DO IT AGAIN.

MAKING BREAD AND OTHER BAKED GOODS MADE ME HAPPY.

THE LOOKS ON PEOPLE'S FACES MADE ME HAPPY TOO.

THE ANTICIPATION!

THE FLAVORS!

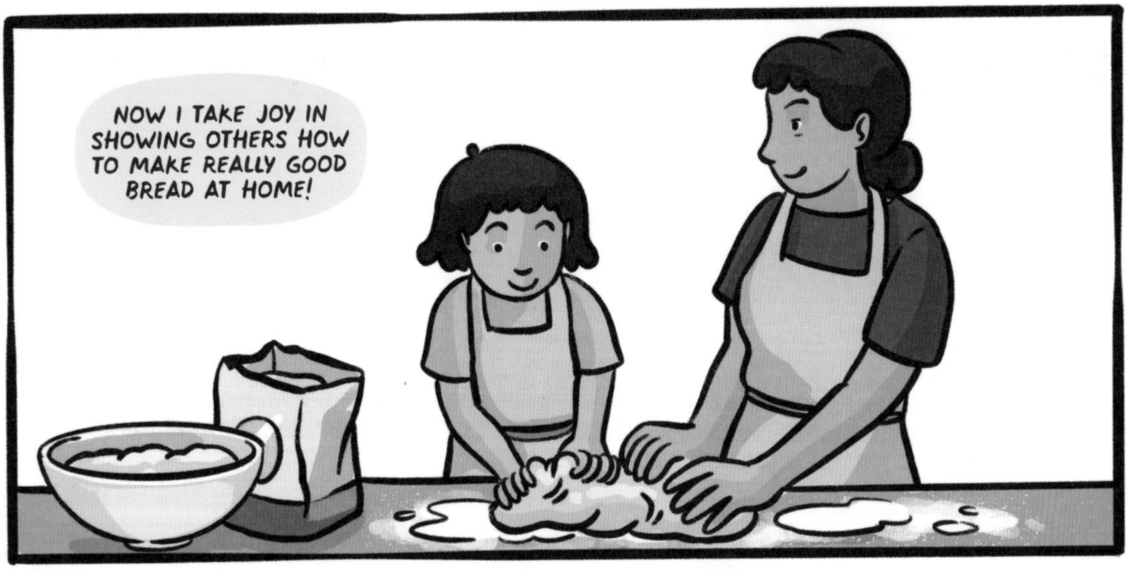
NOW I TAKE JOY IN SHOWING OTHERS HOW TO MAKE REALLY GOOD BREAD AT HOME!

DON'T FORGET!

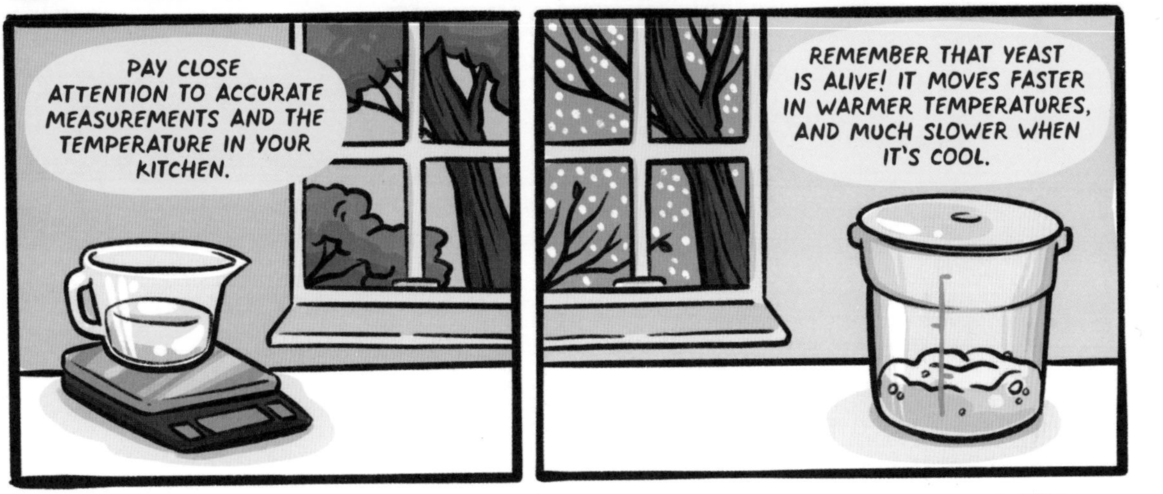
PAY CLOSE ATTENTION TO ACCURATE MEASUREMENTS AND THE TEMPERATURE IN YOUR KITCHEN.
REMEMBER THAT YEAST IS ALIVE! IT MOVES FASTER IN WARMER TEMPERATURES, AND MUCH SLOWER WHEN IT'S COOL.

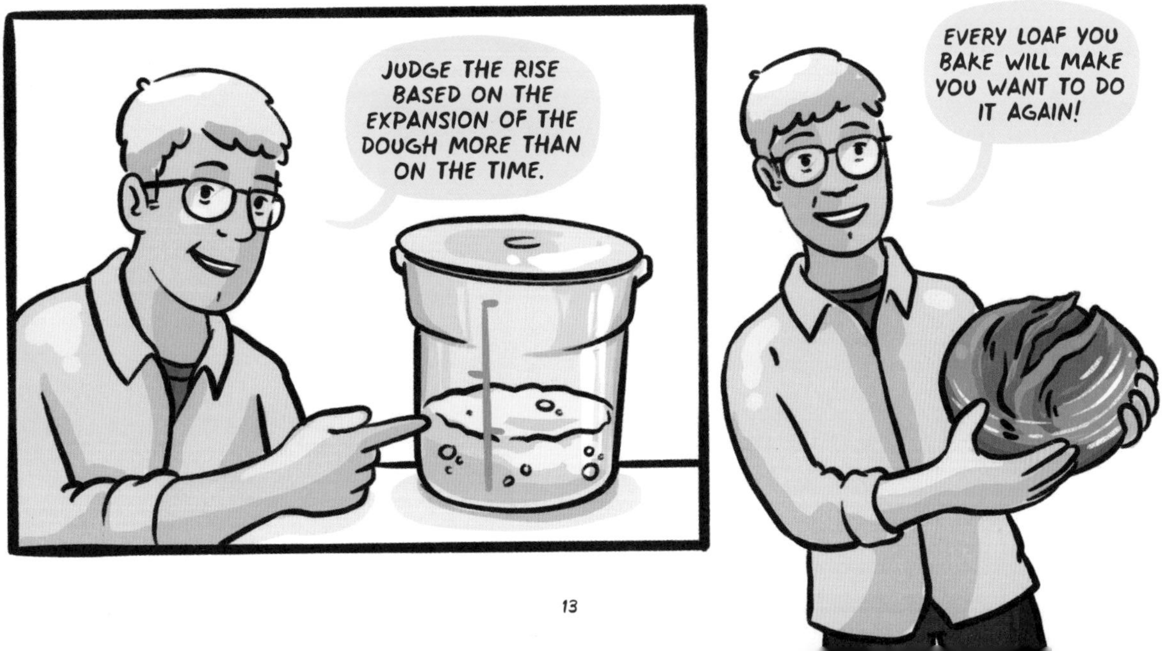
JUDGE THE RISE BASED ON THE EXPANSION OF THE DOUGH MORE THAN ON THE TIME.
EVERY LOAF YOU BAKE WILL MAKE YOU WANT TO DO IT AGAIN!

EQUIPMENT

DOUGH TUB

A 6-QUART ROUND TUB TO MIX THE DOUGH IN AND TO HOLD THE DOUGH AS IT RISES. IT'S BEST TO HAVE A DOUGH TUB WITH VOLUME MARKINGS AND A MATCHING LID. IT MAKES IT EASY TO KNOW FOR SURE WHEN THE DOUGH HAS RISEN TO ITS TARGET POINT.

A LARGE MIXING BOWL CAN SUBSTITUTE FOR THE DOUGH TUB IF YOU CAN COVER IT FAIRLY AIRTIGHT.

SMALLER CONTAINERS

A 2-QUART ROUND TUB WITH A LID IS IDEAL FOR CREATING AND HOLDING YOUR SOURDOUGH CULTURE. YOU'LL WANT A SIMILAR-SIZED VESSEL FOR MEASURING WATER AND FOR WETTING YOUR HAND WHEN YOU MIX AND FOLD THE DOUGH.

DIGITAL PROBE THERMOMETER

TEMPERATURE IS EVERYTHING IN BREAD BAKING. DOUGH RISES MUCH FASTER IN A WARM ROOM, LIKE 80°F, AND MUCH, MUCH SLOWER IN A CHILLY ROOM, SUCH AS 65°F.

AN INSTANT-READ PROBE THERMOMETER LETS YOU MAKE SURE YOU'RE USING THE RIGHT TEMPERATURE OF WATER IN YOUR DOUGH MIX. YOU'LL USE IT TO MEASURE THE TEMPERATURE OF THE DOUGH TOO (JUST STICK THE THERMOMETER INTO THE DOUGH, OR A CONTAINER OF WATER).

DIGITAL KITCHEN SCALE

A DIGITAL KITCHEN SCALE MAKES MEASURING INGREDIENTS EASY AND ACCURATE. IT SHOULD MEASURE UP TO 2 KILOGRAMS (4.4 POUNDS) AND BE ACCURATE TO SINGLE GRAMS.

PROOFING BASKETS FOR DUTCH OVEN LOAVES

PROOFING BASKETS HOLD SHAPED LOAVES AS THEY EXPAND IN THEIR FINAL RISE, CALLED THE PROOF. THIS SIZE WORKS: 9" IN DIAMETER AT THE TOP AND 3 ½" DEEP.

I LIKE CANE PROOFING BASKETS AND LINEN-LINED BASKETS, BUT YOU CAN IMPROVISE BY USING A BOWL OF APPROXIMATELY THE SAME DIMENSIONS LINED WITH A FLOUR-DUSTED, LINT-FREE TEA TOWEL.

BREAD PANS

THE PAN BREAD RECIPES IN THIS BOOK CAN PROBABLY BAKE IN ANY PANS YOU HAVE IN YOUR PANTRY. I USE TWO DIFFERENT PANS: A USA NONSTICK PAN THAT'S 8 ½" BY 4 ½" BY 2 ¾"; OR A SLIGHTLY BIGGER PAN THAT'S 9 ¼" BY 5" BY 3 ⅛". THESE ARE OPEN PANS, WITHOUT LIDS.

I PREFER NONSTICK PANS, BUT I STILL USE COOKING SPRAY. THE LAST THING YOU WANT IS TO HAVE A BEAUTIFUL LOAF OF BREAD YOU CAN'T GET OUT OF THE HOT PAN WHEN IT'S DONE. THAT DRIVES ME NUTS!

DUTCH OVEN

THE DUTCH OVEN SOURDOUGH BREADS IN THIS BOOK ARE BEST BAKED IN A 4-QUART DUTCH OVEN WITH A LID. A BIGGER DUTCH OVEN WILL WORK, BUT THE LOAF WILL BE WIDER AND NOT AS TALL. CAST-IRON DUTCH OVENS WORK JUST AS WELL AS THE FANCY, EXPENSIVE, PRETTIER MODELS.

ODDS AND ENDS

YOU'LL WANT A PAIR OF OVEN MITTS FOR DEALING WITH HOT DUTCH OVENS. MAKE SURE THE MITTS YOU BUY ARE SAFE FOR HANDLING A 500°F POT. ALTERNATIVELY, USE FOLDED KITCHEN TOWELS.

AN OVEN THERMOMETER ALSO COMES IN HANDY, SINCE HOME OVENS RARELY DELIVER THE EXACT TEMPERATURE YOU DIAL IN.

FINALLY, YOU'LL NEED SOMETHING TO COVER THE PROOFING BASKETS AFTER YOU HAVE SHAPED THE LOAVES. I REUSE CLEAN PLASTIC BAGS FROM THE PRODUCE SECTION OF THE MARKET.

INGREDIENTS

YOU CAN MAKE
GREAT BREAD
FROM JUST FOUR
INGREDIENTS:
FLOUR, WATER,
SALT, AND YEAST.

WHITE FLOUR

IF MY RECIPE CALLS FOR WHITE FLOUR,
YOUR SAFEST BET IS TO BUY BAGS
LABELED BREAD FLOUR.

USE THIS HIGHER-PROTEIN FLOUR
(12.5 TO 13 PERCENT PROTEIN CONTENT)
FOR THE TALLEST RISE AND IN RECIPES
THAT COMBINE IT WITH LOW-PROTEIN
FLOURS LIKE RYE, EMMER, EINKORN, AND
SPELT. MANY ALL-PURPOSE FLOURS WORK
FINE WITH THE OTHER RECIPES THAT ARE
PRIMARILY WHITE FLOUR, SUCH AS THE
SATURDAY BREAD AND THE STANDARD, BUT
YOU'LL GET MORE RISE FROM BREAD FLOUR.

TOO BAD THOUGH, PROTEIN CONTENT
IS OFTEN NOT PRINTED ON THE BAG!
IF YOU DO SEE PROTEIN PERCENTAGE
WRITTEN ON THE BAG, THAT'S A GOOD
SIGN THE COMPANY CARES ABOUT
YOUR BREAD BAKING.

IT'S GOOD TO TRY DIFFERENT BRANDS
TO FIND WHICH WORK BEST FOR YOU.
KING ARTHUR BRAND BREAD FLOUR IS
MY CHOICE FOR WHITE FLOUR.

BAKER'S YEAST

YOU MIGHT FIND TWO OR THREE KINDS OF
YEAST AT THE STORE: ACTIVE DRY, RAPID
RISE, AND INSTANT. THE RISE TIMES MAY
VARY A LITTLE BIT BY BRAND, SO PAY
ATTENTION TO THE RECIPE GUIDELINES FOR
VOLUME EXPANSION IN THE DOUGH.

I BUY 16-OUNCE PACKAGES OF SAF RED
INSTANT YEAST, AVAILABLE ONLINE, AND
USE IT FOR ALL OF MY RECIPE TESTING.
IT WILL KEEP FOR A YEAR IF STORED
AIRTIGHT IN THE REFRIGERATOR.

USE ROOM TEMPERATURE FLOUR! DO NOT STORE FLOUR IN THE FRIDGE.

WHOLE-WHEAT FLOUR

WHOLE-WHEAT FLOUR HAS ALL OF THE WHEAT BERRY'S PARTS INCLUDED IN THE FLOUR BAG: THE ENDOSPERM THAT MAKES UP WHITE FLOUR, THE GROUND-UP WHEAT GERM, AND THE GROUND-UP WHEAT BRAN.

IT HAS MORE VITAMINS, MINERALS, AND DIETARY FIBER THAN WHITE FLOUR. THE FLAVOR IS NUTTIER THAN THAT OF WHITE FLOUR, AND BREAD MADE WITH IT WILL BE MORE DENSE THAN ALL-WHITE BREAD.

SALT

USE FINE SEA SALT BECAUSE IT WILL DISSOLVE QUICKLY IN THE DOUGH. DON'T USE IODIZED SALT UNLESS YOU WANT YOUR BREAD TO TASTE LIKE IODINE!

WATER

TAP WATER IS NORMALLY FINE. IF YOUR WATER IS GOOD ENOUGH TO DRINK, IT'S GOOD ENOUGH FOR BAKING.

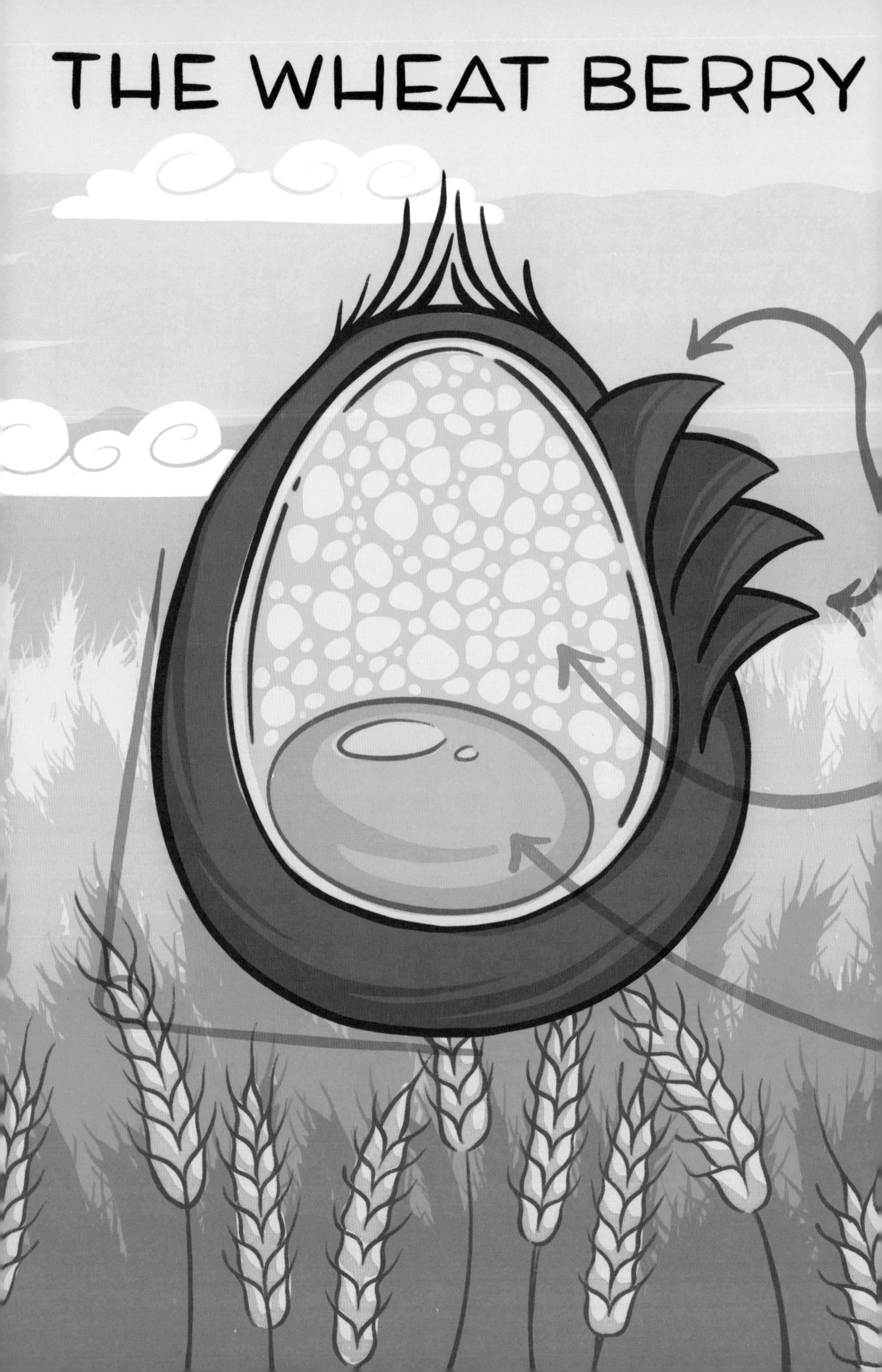
THE WHEAT BERRY

FLOUR

FLOUR IS WHAT YOU GET WHEN WHEAT BERRIES, AKA KERNELS, ARE GROUND INTO A FINE MEAL.

THE KERNEL HAS THREE COMPONENTS, WHICH ARE SEPARATED IN THE MODERN MILLING PROCESS.

WHOLE-WHEAT FLOUR IS MADE FROM THE ENTIRE WHEAT BERRY. WHITE FLOUR IS JUST THE ENDOSPERM.

BRAN

ABOUT 13 PERCENT OF THE WEIGHT OF THE WHEAT BERRY, BRAN IS THE OUTER LAYER OF THE KERNEL. IT CONTAINS MUCH OF WHOLE-WHEAT FLOUR'S DIETARY FIBER AND MOST OF THE MINERAL CONTENT OF THE KERNEL.

ENDOSPERM

THIS IS WHERE WHITE FLOUR COMES FROM. IT EQUALS ABOUT 84 PERCENT OF THE WHEAT BERRY.

GERM

THE COMPONENT OF THE KERNEL THAT CONTAINS THE WHEAT'S GENETIC MATERIAL, THE GERM CONTAINS HEALTHFUL, FLAVORFUL FATS AND MAKES UP ABOUT 3 PERCENT OF THE WEIGHT OF THE KERNEL.

HEIRLOOM GRAINS

IF YOU WANT EVEN TASTIER BREAD, CONSIDER USING HEIRLOOM AND ANCIENT WHEAT VARIETIES.

HEIRLOOM GRAINS ARE NUTTY AND RICH IN FLAVOR!

SOMETIMES THEY'RE CALLED HERITAGE GRAINS. SAME THING!

THESE WHEAT VARIETIES WERE COMMONLY GROWN PRIOR TO THE 1900S.

MANY OLDER TYPES OF REALLY GOOD-TASTING WHEAT WERE LARGELY DISPLACED OVER A CENTURY AGO BY MODERN VARIETIES THAT SCALE BETTER FOR HIGH-VOLUME FARMING.

THE GOAL WAS TO FEED THE PEOPLE, AND THE WHEAT INDUSTRY SUCCEEDED!

BUT FLAVOR SUFFERED.

NOW, MANY SMALLER FARMS GROW THESE TASTY WHEAT CROPS AND MILL THEM INTO FLOUR YOU CAN BAKE WITH.

FLOUR FROM THESE SMALL FARMS IS NOT USUALLY AVAILABLE IN BIG-BOX ONLINE STORES.

MOST SELL ONLINE DIRECTLY TO THE PUBLIC. THE FLOUR YOU BUY WILL BE MILLED FRESH BEFORE IT IS SHIPPED!

WE RECOMMEND CAMAS COUNTRY MILL, JANIE'S MILL, AND CAPAY MILLS, BUT LOOK FOR FAMILY-RUN FARMS NEAR YOU!

YOU ARE NOT LIMITED TO WHAT'S AVAILABLE AT YOUR LOCAL GROCERY STORE, THANKS TO AN ONLINE MARKETPLACE.

YOU CAN SUBSTITUTE HEIRLOOM FLOURS IN MY RECIPES THAT CALL FOR WHOLE-WHEAT FLOUR.

TRY THEM AS THE WHOLE-WHEAT FLOUR IN THESE RECIPES:

WHOLE-WHEAT BREAD, RAISIN-PECAN BREAD, THE STANDARD, MULTIGRAIN BREAD, COUNTRY BREAD, AND WALNUT BREAD.

FRESH-MILLED HEIRLOOM FLOUR IS ALSO AN EXCELLENT CHOICE FOR BUILDING YOUR OWN SOURDOUGH, AS IT IS HIGH IN NUTRIENTS TO FEED THE CULTURE.

THE SETUP

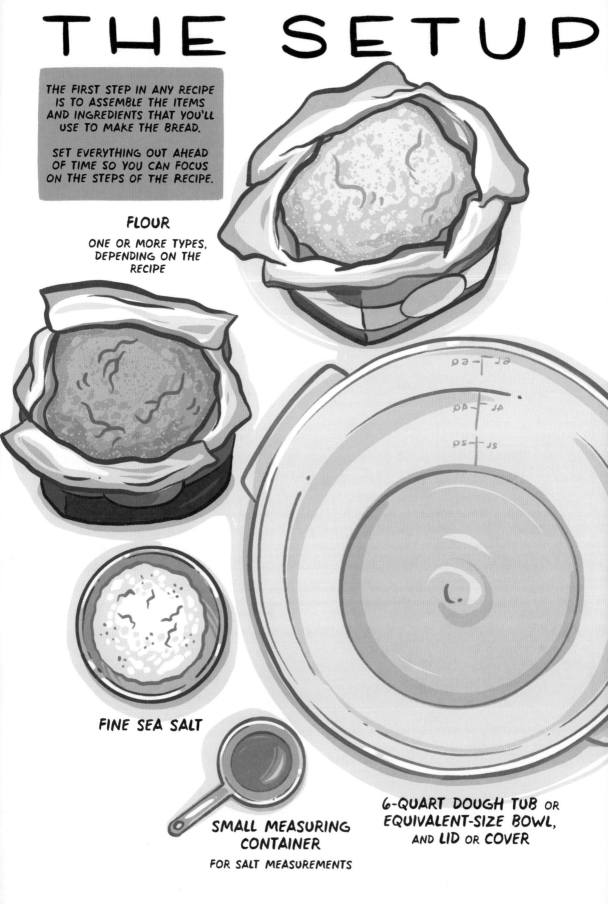

THE FIRST STEP IN ANY RECIPE IS TO ASSEMBLE THE ITEMS AND INGREDIENTS THAT YOU'LL USE TO MAKE THE BREAD.

SET EVERYTHING OUT AHEAD OF TIME SO YOU CAN FOCUS ON THE STEPS OF THE RECIPE.

FLOUR
ONE OR MORE TYPES, DEPENDING ON THE RECIPE

FINE SEA SALT

SMALL MEASURING CONTAINER
FOR SALT MEASUREMENTS

6-QUART DOUGH TUB OR **EQUIVALENT-SIZE BOWL,** AND **LID** OR **COVER**

INSTANT DRIED YEAST

¼ TEASPOON
TO MEASURE SMALL
AMOUNTS OF YEAST

PROOFING BASKET
IF BAKING A
DUTCH OVEN LOAF

DIGITAL PROBE
THERMOMETER
TO MEASURE
TEMPERATURES

LEVAIN OR
STARTER

WATER CONTAINER
2-QUART OR LARGER

DIGITAL
KITCHEN SCALE

ABOUT THESE
WET, SLACK DOUGHS

MY BREAD DOUGH HAS MORE WATER IN IT THAN YOU MIGHT BE USED TO. IT'S WET AND GOOPY AT FIRST.

WATER IN THE DOUGH TURNS INTO STEAM AS THE BREAD BAKES.

THE STEAM EXPANDS THE DOUGH AND MAKES SMALL HOLES OR BIG HOLES ON THE INSIDE, DEPENDING ON THE BREAD AND HOW YOU MAKE IT.

I USE A TECHNIQUE CALLED FOLDING THE DOUGH DURING THE FIRST RISE.

FOLDING HELPS THE DOUGH BUILD UP ENOUGH STRUCTURE TO HOLD THE RISE AND BAKE WITHOUT COLLAPSING.

IT FEELS WEIRD THE FIRST COUPLE OF TIMES.

IF YOU USE A SCALE TO ACCURATELY MEASURE FLOUR AND WATER, IT'LL BE ALL RIGHT.

SOME NOTES ABOUT
TEMPERATURE & SEASON

FOR THE BREAD TO BAKE TO ITS FULL SIZE AND HAVE THAT WONDERFUL LIGHT AND OPEN CRUMB, YOU NEED COMPLETE FERMENTATION OF THE DOUGH.

AFTER MIXING, YOU'LL LET THE DOUGH RISE IN ITS DOUGH TUB UNTIL IT HAS INCREASED IN VOLUME ABOUT TWO AND A HALF TIMES.

WARMER TEMPERATURES ACCELERATE THE METABOLIC RATE OF THE YEAST AND OTHER ORGANIC COMPONENTS IN THE DOUGH ...

WHICH MAKES IT RISE FASTER.

IN MY HOUSE IN HAWAII, AT 80°F, IT TAKES ABOUT 2 HOURS FOR THE DOUGH TO FULLY RISE.

COOLER TEMPERATURES WILL SLOW DOWN THIS ACTIVITY.

IN MY APARTMENT IN CHICAGO, IT'S ONLY 65°F IN THE WINTER. IT CAN TAKE 4 TO 5 HOURS TO RISE TO THE SAME POINT!

LET THE AMOUNT OF TOTAL RISE, RATHER THAN THE RISE TIME, INDICATE WHEN TO REMOVE THE DOUGH FROM ITS CONTAINER AND MAKE UP YOUR LOAF.

FIND A WARM SPOT!

BASIC BREAD METHOD IN EIGHT STEPS

THE BAKER'S TERM FOR THIS INITIAL MIX OF THE DOUGH IS "AUTOLYSE."

IT MEANS YOU MIX THE FLOUR AND WATER AND LET IT REST FOR 15 TO 20 MINUTES BEFORE MIXING IN THE SALT AND YEAST.

FILL A 2-QUART CONTAINER ABOUT TWO-THIRDS FULL WITH WATER AT A GUESSED-AT 90°F.

MEASURE THE TEMPERATURE WITH YOUR DIGITAL PROBE THERMOMETER . . .

ADDING HOTTER OR COLDER WATER . . .

UNTIL YOU GET IT CLOSE.

WEIGH THE WATER FOR THE RECIPE. PUT YOUR EMPTY DOUGH TUB ON A SCALE . . .

AND PRESS "TARE" OR "ZERO" TO START AT 0.

POUR THE WARM WATER INTO THE 6-QUART DOUGH TUB TO REACH THE WEIGHT OF WATER SPECIFIED IN THE RECIPE.

IF YOU HAVE A LEVAIN (SEE PAGE 44) YOU WILL NEED TO SCALE IT INTO THE DOUGH TUB WITH THE WATER BEFORE ADDING FLOUR.

FIRST, HIT "TARE" OR "ZERO" ON THE SCALE.

POUR THE CULTURE INTO THE WATER UNTIL YOU REACH THE WEIGHT THE RECIPE CALLS FOR.

THEN, PINCH THE FLOW WITH WET FINGERS TO STOP IT.

STIR THE LEVAIN WITH YOUR FINGERS AND SWOOSH IT AROUND TO BLEND IT WITH THE WATER A BIT.

KEEP THE TUB ON THE SCALE, HIT "TARE" OR "ZERO" AGAIN . . .

AND ADD ALL THE FLOUR PER THE AMOUNT(S) IN THE RECIPE.

HOLD THE TUB WITH ONE HAND AND USE YOUR DOMINANT HAND TO MIX THE FLOUR AND WATER INTO A DOUGH.

YOU WILL KNOW THIS STEP IS DONE WHEN THERE ARE NO LONGER ANY LOOSE BITS OF DRY FLOUR VISIBLE IN THE DOUGH TUB.

YOUR WORKING HAND WILL GET A LITTLE STICKY WITH DOUGH. DON'T WORRY — YOU ARE A BAKER NOW!

AFTER MIXING, USE YOUR FREE HAND TO SQUEEGEE THE DOUGH THAT'S STUCK TO YOUR WORKING HAND INTO THE TUB.

MEASURE THE FINE SEA SALT ON YOUR SCALE. PLACE AN EMPTY CONTAINER ON THE SCALE, AND HIT "TARE" OR "ZERO."

ADD SALT UNTIL YOU HIT THE SPECIFIED WEIGHT.

AND SPRINKLE THE SALT EVENLY OVER THE WET DOUGH. (IT WILL PARTIALLY DISSOLVE.)

REPEAT THIS STEP WITH THE DRY YEAST. DON'T FREAK OUT IF THE SALT AND YEAST ARE IN CONTACT, IT'S NOTHING TO WORRY ABOUT.

LET REST, COVERED, FOR ABOUT 15 MINUTES.

STEP 2: FINAL DOUGH MIX

FOR THE FINAL MIX OF THE DOUGH, YOU'LL WANT TO WORK WITH A WET HAND SO THE DOUGH DOESN'T STICK TO YOUR HANDS.

SET UP A CONTAINER WITH WARM WATER NEXT TO YOU.

DIP YOUR WORKING HAND INTO THE WATER AND GRAB THE DOUGH TUB BY THE RIM WITH YOUR OTHER HAND.

REACH UNDERNEATH THE DOUGH WITH YOUR WET HAND AND GRAB A SECTION OF IT, ABOUT ONE-FOURTH OF THE WHOLE MASS.

NOW LET'S ENCLOSE THE SALT AND YEAST!

APPLY PRESSURE WITH THE FLAT PARTS OF YOUR HAND AND FINGERS, NOT YOUR FINGERTIPS.

GENTLY PULL IT OUT AND UP . . .

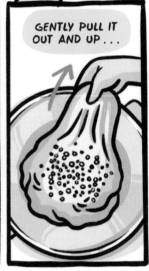

AND THEN FOLD IT OVER THE TOP TO THE OTHER SIDE OF THE DOUGH.

REPEAT 3 MORE TIMES WITH THE REMAINING DOUGH . . .

UNTIL THE SALT AND YEAST ARE FULLY ENCLOSED.

THE PINCER METHOD!

WITH A WET WORKING HAND, USE A PINCERLIKE GRIP WITH YOUR THUMB AND FOREFINGER . . .

AND SQUEEZE BIG CHUNKS OF DOUGH AND THEN TIGHTEN YOUR GRIP TO CUT THROUGH IT.

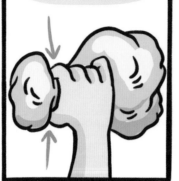

REPEAT, CUTTING 5 OR 6 TIMES THROUGH THE DOUGH.

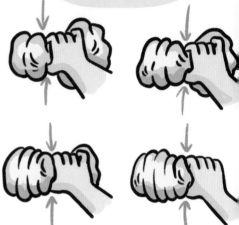

STRETCH AND FOLD THE DOUGH OVER ITSELF FROM ALL ANGLES.

REPEAT THE CUT-AND-FOLD STEPS SEVERAL TIMES, DIPPING YOUR WORKING HAND BACK INTO THE WARM WATER AS NEEDED TO PREVENT THE DOUGH FROM STICKING TO YOU.

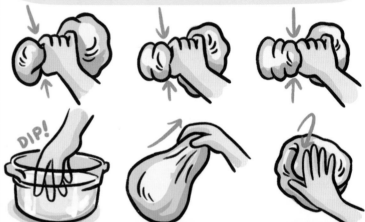

DIP!

A FEW MINUTES OF THIS CUT-AND-FOLD PROCESS WILL BE FINE. THAT'S IT FOR MIXING!

MEASURE THE TEMPERATURE OF THE DOUGH WITH YOUR PROBE THERMOMETER.

YOUR TARGET TEMPERATURE IS ABOUT 75°F / 24°C. A LITTLE VARIANCE IS FINE.

IF YOUR DOUGH IS MUCH WARMER IT WILL RISE FASTER, AND IF IT'S MUCH COOLER THE RISE WILL TAKE LONGER.

BECAUSE MY DOUGHS ARE WET AND LOOSE, THEY NEED A LITTLE HELP.

FOLDING THE DOUGH HELPS DEVELOP THE GLUTEN THAT GIVES THE DOUGH ITS STRENGTH AND CONTRIBUTES TO GOOD VOLUME IN THE FINAL LOAF.

THE RECIPES IN THIS BOOK NEED JUST 2 OR 3 FOLDS.

DO YOUR FIRST DOUGH FOLD ABOUT 10 MINUTES AFTER THE DOUGH IS MIXED.

YOU'LL KNOW WHEN TO FOLD AGAIN: IN TIME IT GOES FROM BEING A BALL WITH STRUCTURE . . .

TO LYING FLATTENED OUT IN THE TUB. THAT'S WHEN YOU FOLD IT AGAIN.

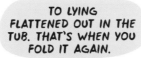

TO BEGIN FOLDING, WET YOUR HAND SO THE DOUGH DOESN'T STICK TO YOU.

WITH YOUR WET HAND, REACH UNDERNEATH THE DOUGH AND PULL ABOUT ONE-FOURTH OF IT OUT AND UP TO STRETCH IT AS FAR AS YOU CAN UNTIL YOU FEEL RESISTANCE.

THEN FOLD IT OVER THE TOP TO THE OTHER SIDE OF THE DOUGH.

REPEAT 4 OR 5 TIMES, WORKING AROUND THE DOUGH UNTIL IT HAS TIGHTENED INTO A BALL.

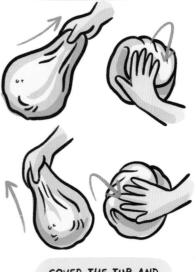

COVER THE TUB AND LET THE DOUGH RISE.

STEP 4: REMOVE THE DOUGH FROM ITS TUB

WHEN THE DOUGH HAS RISEN TO JUST SHY OF THE 2-QUART LINE (ABOUT ¼ INCH), IT'S READY TO BE REMOVED!

REMEMBER: THIS HAPPENS FASTER WHEN IT'S IN A WARM ROOM, AND TAKES LONGER WHEN IT'S IN A COLDER ROOM.

MODERATELY FLOUR A WORK SURFACE ABOUT 12 INCHES WIDE.

YOU'LL NEED TO CAREFULLY REMOVE THE DOUGH IN ONE PIECE. HERE'S HOW:

FLOUR YOUR HANDS.

BEING CAREFUL NOT TO TEAR THE DOUGH . . .

WORK SOME FLOUR ALONG THE EDGES OF THE DOUGH . . .

AND THEN UNDERNEATH IT, AS YOU SLOWLY REMOVE THE DOUGH FROM THE TUB.

GENTLY EASE THE DOUGH OUT ONTO THE FLOURED WORK SURFACE.

STEP 5: SHAPE THE LOAF

FOR OPEN PAN LOAVES

FIRST, SPRITZ YOUR BAKING PAN WITH COOKING SPRAY.

FLOUR YOUR HANDS.

DON'T STRESS ABOUT THIS PART! THE PAN WILL DO MOST OF THE WORK FOR YOU.

GRAB THE DOUGH FROM UNDERNEATH AND STRETCH IT LEFT AND RIGHT UNTIL IT RESISTS.

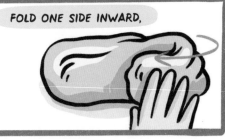

FOLD ONE SIDE INWARD,

THEN FOLD THE OTHER SIDE OVER TO ABOUT THE WIDTH OF THE PAN.

ROLL IT UP FROM THE BOTTOM UP OR FROM TOP TO BOTTOM TO FORM A TUBE OF DOUGH.

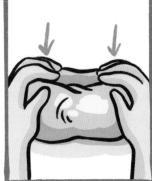

GENTLY PULL THE DOUGH BACK TOWARD YOU TO TIGHTEN IT UP A BIT.

PLACE THE DOUGH SEAM SIDE UP INTO THE PAN.

SHAPING A LOAF WELL TAKES PRACTICE. YOU'LL IMPROVE YOUR SHAPING WITH EACH LOAF YOU MAKE!

FOR DUTCH OVEN LOAVES

USE THE SAME TECHNIQUE AS IN THE FOLDING STEP, BUT THIS TIME WITH LIGHTLY FLOURED HANDS.

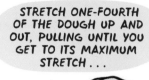
STRETCH ONE-FOURTH OF THE DOUGH UP AND OUT, PULLING UNTIL YOU GET TO ITS MAXIMUM STRETCH . . .

AND FOLD IT OVER THE TOP OF THE DOUGH.

REPEAT, ALL AROUND THE DOUGH, FORMING IT INTO A BALL.

ON A CLEAN, DRY, UNFLOURED SURFACE, FLIP THE ROUND OVER SO THE SEAM IS ON THE BOTTOM.

CUP YOUR HANDS AROUND THE BACK OF THE DOUGH BALL.

APPLY ENOUGH DOWNWARD PRESSURE SO THE DOUGH BALL GRIPS YOUR WORK SURFACE A BIT.

LEADING WITH YOUR PINKIE FINGERS, PULL THE ENTIRE DOUGH BALL 6 TO 8 INCHES TOWARD YOU.

GIVE THE LOAF A QUARTER TURN AND REPEAT THIS TIGHTENING STEP UNTIL YOU'VE GONE ALL THE WAY AROUND THE DOUGH BALL 2 OR 3 TIMES.

THIS WILL TIGHTEN UP THE BALL AND ADD TENSION TO IT.

PLACE YOUR SHAPED LOAF SEAM SIDE DOWN IN A GENEROUSLY FLOURED PROOFING BASKET.

34

STEP 6: PROOF

THE SECOND RISE IS CALLED THE PROOF.

TIME AND TEMPERATURE ARE THE TWO THINGS THAT DETERMINE HOW LONG TO LET YOUR SHAPED LOAF RISE BEFORE IT'S READY TO BAKE.

IF IT TAKES 1 HOUR AT ROOM TEMPERATURE, IT CAN TAKE 12 HOURS OR MORE IF HELD THE ENTIRE TIME IN THE REFRIGERATOR.

FOR OPEN PAN LOAVES

FIRST, COVER THE LOAF TO KEEP IT FROM DRYING OUT.

USING YOUR HAND, SPREAD A THIN FILM OF WATER OVER THE ENTIRE TOP OF THE LOAF TO KEEP THE DOUGH FROM STICKING TO THE BAG.

PLACE YOUR BREAD PAN IN A PLASTIC BAG, LEAVING IT LOOSE AT THE TOP SO THE DOUGH CAN EXPAND.

IT DOESN'T NEED TO BE AIRTIGHT. THE POINT OF THE BAG IS TO KEEP THE DOUGH FROM DRYING OUT DURING THE PROOF TIME.

OR YOU COULD INSTEAD COVER THE LOAF LOOSELY WITH PLASTIC WRAP. IT WILL PEEL OFF EASILY IF YOU APPLIED THE FILM OF WATER.

WHEN IT'S DONE PROOFING, THE DOUGH SHOULD INFLATE A BIT ABOVE THE PAN RIM, AND SHOULD LOOK SLIGHTLY DOMED IN THE MIDDLE.

REMEMBER TO LET YOUR OVEN PREHEAT FOR 45 MINUTES OR SO BEFORE BAKING, AND BUILD THAT TIME INTO YOUR PROOFING TIME!

FOR DUTCH OVEN LOAVES

LIKE WITH OPEN PAN LOAVES, THE GOAL IS TO KEEP THE DOUGH FROM DRYING OUT WHILE IT IS PROOFING.

PUT YOUR PROOFING BASKET IN A PLASTIC BAG WHILE YOU WAIT FOR THE DOUGH TO PROOF. IT DOESN'T NEED TO BE AIRTIGHT.

HOW DO YOU KNOW WHEN A LOAF IS DONE PROOFING?

THE FINGER-DENT TEST IS THE MOST FOOLPROOF METHOD THAT I KNOW!

POKE THE RISING LOAF WITH A FLOURED FINGER, MAKING AN INDENTATION ABOUT ½" DEEP.

IF IT SPRINGS BACK IMMEDIATELY, THE LOAF NEEDS MORE PROOFING TIME.

IF IT SPRINGS BACK SLOWLY AND INCOMPLETELY, THE LOAF IS FULLY PROOFED AND READY TO BAKE.

IF IT DOESN'T SPRING BACK AT ALL, THE LOAF MAY BE A LITTLE PAST ITS PRIME POINT FOR BAKING.

IF IT'S OVERPROOFED, DON'T PANIC! GO AHEAD AND BAKE, KNOWING THE LOAF MAY COLLAPSE A BIT.

BUT IT MIGHT NOT! I'M SOMETIMES SURPRISED TO FIND THAT A LOAF I THOUGHT OVERPROOFED HOLDS ITS FORM AND BAKES UP JUST FINE.

STEP 7: PREHEAT

FOR OPEN PAN LOAVES

FOR DUTCH OVEN LOAVES

WE PREHEAT FOR A BIT LONGER TO MAKE SURE THE OVEN IS SATURATED WITH HEAT.

ABOUT 45 MINUTES PRIOR TO BAKING, POSITION A RACK IN THE MIDDLE OF THE OVEN AND PREHEAT THE OVEN TO 450°F / 230°C.

POSITION A RACK IN THE MIDDLE OF THE OVEN. PUT YOUR EMPTY 4-QUART DUTCH OVEN, WITH THE LID, ON THE MIDDLE RACK. PREHEAT THE OVEN TO 475°F / 245°C FOR 45 MINUTES.

SOMETIMES, DEPENDING ON THE OVEN, THE BREAD LOOKS GOOD ON TOP BUT ENDS UP SCORCHED ON THE BOTTOM.

IF THIS IS A PROBLEM, MAKE SURE YOUR DUTCH OVEN IS ON A MIDDLE RACK IN YOUR OVEN, AS HIGH ABOVE THE HEATING ELEMENT AS IT WILL FIT.

POSITION ANOTHER RACK ON THE NEXT-LOWEST RUNG.

ABOUT 30 MINUTES INTO THE BAKE, SLIDE A CAST-IRON SKILLET OR A SHEET PAN ON THE LOWER RACK DIRECTLY BENEATH THE DUTCH OVEN. THIS WILL ACT AS A HEAT SHIELD.

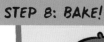

STEP 8: BAKE!

FOR OPEN PAN LOAVES

PUT YOUR PAN INTO THE OVEN ON THE CENTER OF THE MIDDLE RACK . . .

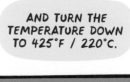

AND TURN THE TEMPERATURE DOWN TO 425°F / 220°C.

A BAKE TIME OF 50 MINUTES IS IDEAL FOR THE OPEN PAN BREAD RECIPES, BUT IT'S ALWAYS GOOD TO CHECK AT AROUND 40 MINUTES.

THE TOP OF THE PAN LOAF BAKES TO A MUCH DARKER COLOR THAN THE SIDES AND BOTTOM.

IF YOU THINK IT'S DONE WHEN THE TOP IS LIGHT BROWN, YOU'LL DISCOVER THE SIDES ARE BAKED TOO LIGHT, AND THE LOAF MAY COLLAPSE ON ITSELF.

BAKE UNTIL THE TOP IS DARK BROWN, AND THE REST OF THE LOAF WILL BE GOLDEN COLORED.

IF YOU USED COOKING SPRAY, THE LOAF SHOULD POP RIGHT OUT OF THE PAN.

BUT SOMETIMES THE EDGES OF THE LOAF OVERLAP THE SIDES OF SMALLER BREAD PANS, AND THE LOAF BECOMES A LITTLE BIT STUCK.

WITH OVEN MITTS OR KITCHEN TOWELS PROTECTING YOUR HANDS, RAP THE BREAD PAN FORCEFULLY ON A HARD SURFACE THAT WON'T BE DAMAGED.

IF THAT DOESN'T DO THE TRICK, GRAB THE EDGE OF THE PAN WITH ONE HAND (PROTECTED BY A FOLDED KITCHEN TOWEL) AND PRY OUT THE LOAF WITH YOUR OTHER HAND.

SOUNDS KLUDGY, BUT IF YOU HAVE A NONSTICK PAN IT WILL COME OUT WITH SOME PRYING.

LET THE LOAF COOL ON A WIRE RACK, SO AIR CAN FLOW AROUND IT.

FOR DUTCH OVEN LOAVES

WEAR OVEN MITTS TO PROTECT YOU FROM THE HEAT OF THE DUTCH OVEN AND ITS LID!

CAREFULLY REMOVE THE DUTCH OVEN FROM THE *OVEN* OVEN.

INVERT THE PROOFING BASKET ONTO A FLOURED COUNTERTOP.

IF THE LOAF STICKS TO THE EDGES OF THE PROOFING BASKET, USE ONE HAND TO DELICATELY RELEASE THE DOUGH . . .

AND MAKE A MENTAL NOTE THAT YOU NEED TO DUST THE BASKET WITH MORE FLOUR NEXT TIME. NEW WICKER BASKETS NEED MORE FLOUR THAN SEASONED BASKETS.

IF THE DOUGH STILL STICKS TO THE BASKET, THEN IT MIGHT BE TOO STICKY. NEXT TIME, CUT BACK THE WATER IN THE RECIPE BY 20 OR 30 GRAMS.

OR IT COULD BE THAT YOU NEED TO WORK ON HOW YOU SHAPE THE LOAF.

STICKY

FLOUR

MAKE SURE YOU FOLD THE DRY, FLOUR-DUSTED SIDE OF THE DOUGH OVER THE STICKY INTERIOR PART WHEN YOU FORM THE ROUND — AND GIVE IT SOME TENSION AS YOU SHAPE IT.

NEXT, USE THE MITTS TO REMOVE THE DUTCH OVEN LID.

USE THE BROAD PART OF YOUR HANDS AND FINGERS, NOT YOUR FINGERTIPS, TO PICK UP THE LOAF . . .

AND VERY CAREFULLY PLACE THE LOAF IN THE HOT DUTCH OVEN.

USE THE MITTS TO PUT THE LID ON THE DUTCH OVEN . . .

AND RETURN IT TO THE CENTER OF THE MIDDLE RACK OF THE PREHEATED OVEN.

SET A TIMER FOR 30 MINUTES.

AFTER 30 MINUTES, REMOVE THE LID.

THE LOAF WILL BE FULLY RISEN. THERE SHOULD BE ONE OR MORE ATTRACTIVE SPLITS IN THE TOP WHERE THE DOUGH EXPANDED, AND THE CRUST SHOULD BE A LIGHT GOLD.

SET THE TIMER FOR ANOTHER 20 MINUTES AND CONTINUE BAKING, LID OFF.

BAKE UNTIL THE LOAF IS DARK BROWN ALL AROUND. TOTAL BAKING TIME SHOULD BE ABOUT 50 MINUTES.

REMOVE THE DUTCH OVEN FROM YOUR OVEN, AND TILT THE POT TO TURN OUT THE LOAF.

LET THE LOAF COOL ON A WIRE RACK OR ON ITS SIDE FOR 20 TO 30 MINUTES BEFORE SLICING.

THE INSIDE OF THE LOAF CONTINUES TO BAKE AFTER IT'S REMOVED FROM THE OVEN, AND IT NEEDS THAT TIME TO FINISH.

SNAP!

ENJOY THE CRACKLING SOUND OF THE COOLING BREAD!

CRACKLE!

CRACK!

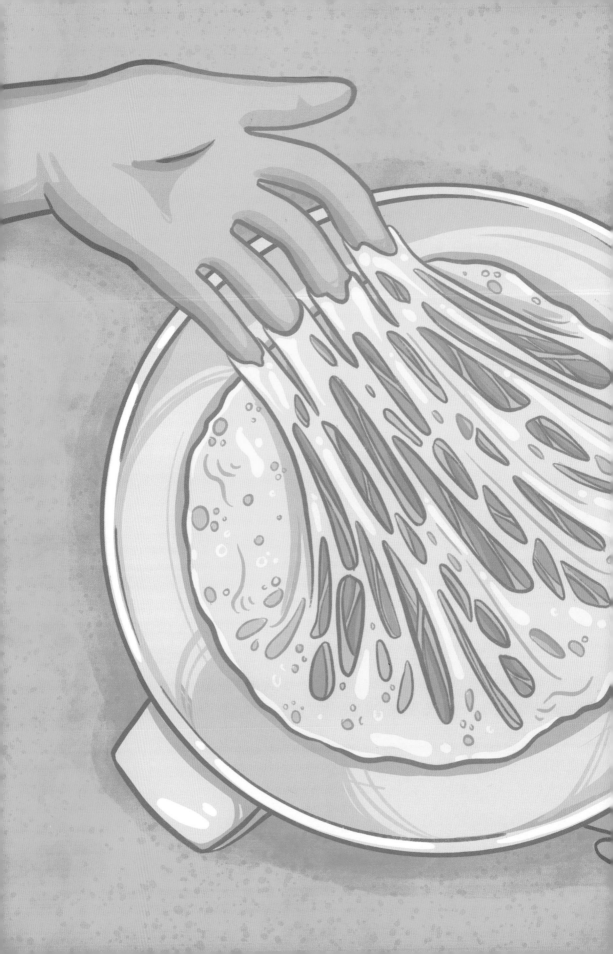

LEVAIN

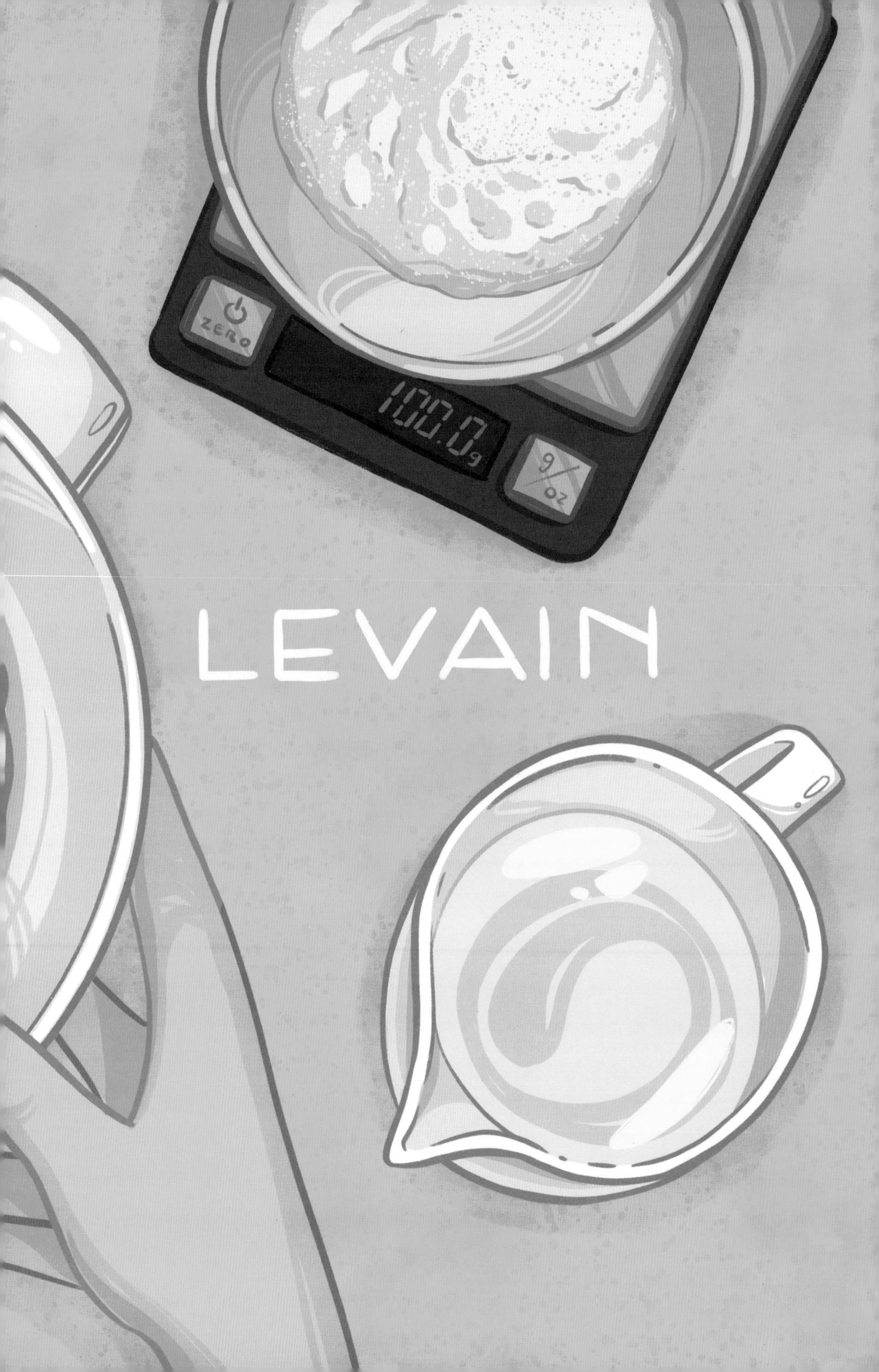
ZERO
100.0g
g/oz

LEVAIN = SOURDOUGH

"LEVAIN" IS THE FRENCH WORD FOR "SOURDOUGH."

BECAUSE I DON'T WANT MY BREADS TO TASTE SOUR, I USUALLY USE THE WORD "LEVAIN."

BOTH WORDS MEAN THE SAME THING: A WILD-YEAST CULTURE MADE UP FROM MANY FEEDINGS OF JUST FLOUR AND WATER . . .

THAT MAKES YOUR DOUGH RISE AND MAKES THE BREAD TASTE GOOD.

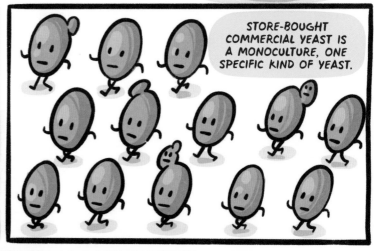

STORE-BOUGHT COMMERCIAL YEAST IS A MONOCULTURE, ONE SPECIFIC KIND OF YEAST.

A LEVAIN CULTURE HOSTS MULTIPLE VARIETIES OF YEASTS THAT OCCUR NATURALLY. THEY ARE IN THE AIR AND IN YOUR FLOUR.

BECAUSE OF THIS MORE COMPLEX BIOLOGY, BREADS MADE FROM YOUR LEVAIN WILL HAVE A MORE COMPLEX FLAVOR.

THEY ALSO TAKE LONGER TO GO STALE!

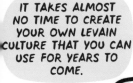

IT TAKES ALMOST NO TIME TO CREATE YOUR OWN LEVAIN CULTURE THAT YOU CAN USE FOR YEARS TO COME.

TO DO THIS, MIX WHOLE-GRAIN FLOUR AND WATER...

LET IT SIT OUT FOR A DAY IN A WARM SPOT...

AND WITHIN 24 HOURS IT STARTS TO SHOW SMALL BUBBLES!

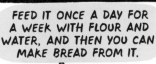

FEED IT ONCE A DAY FOR A WEEK WITH FLOUR AND WATER, AND THEN YOU CAN MAKE BREAD FROM IT.

STORE IT IN THE FRIDGE, REFRESH IT ROUGHLY ONCE A WEEK...

AND PLUCK FROM IT WHENEVER YOU NEED IT FOR A RECIPE.

THAT'S SOURDOUGH.

IT'S FUNKY! IT'S FULL OF YEAST!

IT'S ALIVE AND IT NEEDS TO BE FED!

FEED ME!

STARTING YOUR LEVAIN

TO START YOUR LEVAIN, YOU WILL NEED THESE THINGS OVER THE NEXT 7 DAYS:

STONE-MILLED HEIRLOOM WHEAT IS GREAT FOR THIS!

250 GRAMS WHOLE-WHEAT FLOUR

WATER

CONTAINER WITH LID (A 2-QUART TUB IS A GOOD SIZE)

DIGITAL PROBE THERMOMETER

DIGITAL KITCHEN SCALE

400 GRAMS WHITE FLOUR (ALL-PURPOSE OR BREAD FLOUR IS FINE)

DAY 1

MEASURE THE WEIGHT OF THE EMPTY CONTAINER YOU WILL USE TO MAKE YOUR SOURDOUGH.

WRITE IT ON THE SIDE OF THE CONTAINER. YOU'LL NEED THIS LATER!

BY HAND, MIX 50 GRAMS WHOLE-WHEAT FLOUR WITH 50 GRAMS (95° TO 100°F / 35° TO 38°C) WATER.

LET IT SIT OUT UNCOVERED FOR AN HOUR OR TWO . . .

THEN PUT THE LID ON IT.

LEAVE IT OUT AT ROOM TEMPERATURE OVERNIGHT — 68° TO 70°F / 20° TO 21°C IS FINE.

DAY 2 (ROUGHLY 24 HOURS LATER)

ADD 50 GRAMS WHOLE-WHEAT FLOUR AND 50 GRAMS (95° TO 100°F / 35° TO 38°C) WATER TO WHAT YOU MADE YESTERDAY . . .

AND MIX BY HAND.

PUT THE LID ON IT. DO NOT REFRIGERATE.

DAY 3 (ROUGHLY 24 HOURS LATER)

THE NEW CULTURE SHOULD BE GASSY AND ALIVE!

ADD 50 GRAMS WHOLE-WHEAT FLOUR AND 50 GRAMS (95° TO 100°F / 35° TO 38°C) WATER AND MIX BY HAND.

50G

50G
95°F

PUT THE LID ON IT. DO NOT REFRIGERATE.

DAY 4 (ROUGHLY 24 HOURS LATER)

AT THIS POINT, IF YOUR CULTURE IS NOT SHOWING ANY SIGNS OF LIFE BEFORE ITS FEEDING, SOMETHING'S WRONG.

IF THAT'S THE CASE, YOU SHOULD STOP, THROW IT AWAY, AND TRY AGAIN WITH A DIFFERENT BRAND OF WHOLE-WHEAT FLOUR.

THIS TIME, ADD 100 GRAMS WHOLE-WHEAT FLOUR AND 100 GRAMS (95° TO 100°F / 35° TO 38°C) WATER AND MIX BY HAND.

100G

100G
95°F

PUT THE LID ON IT. DO NOT REFRIGERATE.

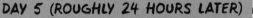

DAY 5 (ROUGHLY 24 HOURS LATER)

IT'S A CARBONATED, ALCOHOLIC WEB OF LIVELY CULTURE! HOORAY!

NOW WE'LL SWITCH TO WHITE FLOUR.

CHECK THE EMPTY WEIGHT OF YOUR CONTAINER THAT YOU WROTE DOWN BEFORE YOU STARTED.

THIS PART IS A LITTLE MESSY, SO KEEP A KITCHEN TOWEL NEARBY, USE A WET HAND, AND HAVE YOUR SCALE AND A TRASH CAN RIGHT THERE.

DUMP THE MIXTURE UNTIL 100 GRAMS REMAINS.

131
+100
=231

ADD 100 GRAMS WHITE FLOUR AND 100 GRAMS (85°F / 29°C) WATER. MIX BY HAND.

100G
100G
85°F

PUT THE LID ON IT AND LET IT SIT OUT OVERNIGHT.

DAY 6 (ROUGHLY 24 HOURS LATER)

THIS NEW CULTURE SHOULD NOW BE VERY GASSY AND FRAGRANT.

YOU SHOULD SMELL ITS LEATHERY AROMAS AND GET AN AROMATIC HINT OF ITS ACIDITY TOO.

REMOVE AND TOSS ALL BUT 50 GRAMS OF CULTURE.

ADD 100 GRAMS WHITE FLOUR AND 100 GRAMS (80°F / 27°C) WATER. MIX BY HAND.

COVER AND LET IT SIT OUT FOR 24 HOURS.

DAY 7 (ROUGHLY 24 HOURS LATER)

THE CULTURE IS ALMOST READY TO MAKE UP YOUR LONG-TERM LEVAIN!

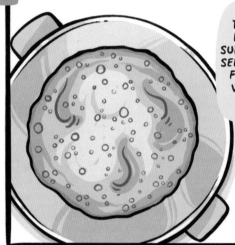

BEFORE THIS FEEDING, IT SHOULD BE SUPER-GASSY AND SEEM FULLY ALIVE, FIZZY ALMOST, WITH A LITTLE BIT OF FROTH ON THE TOP.

WHEN YOU REACH YOUR WET HAND INTO IT TO DISCARD THE EXCESS, IT SHOULD FEEL LIGHT AND AIRY, WITH A DELICATE WEBBING.

IT SHOULD HAVE A MELLOW, COMPLEX, LACTIC-ALCOHOL SMELL OF FERMENTATION WITH A HINT OF BACKGROUND ACIDITY.

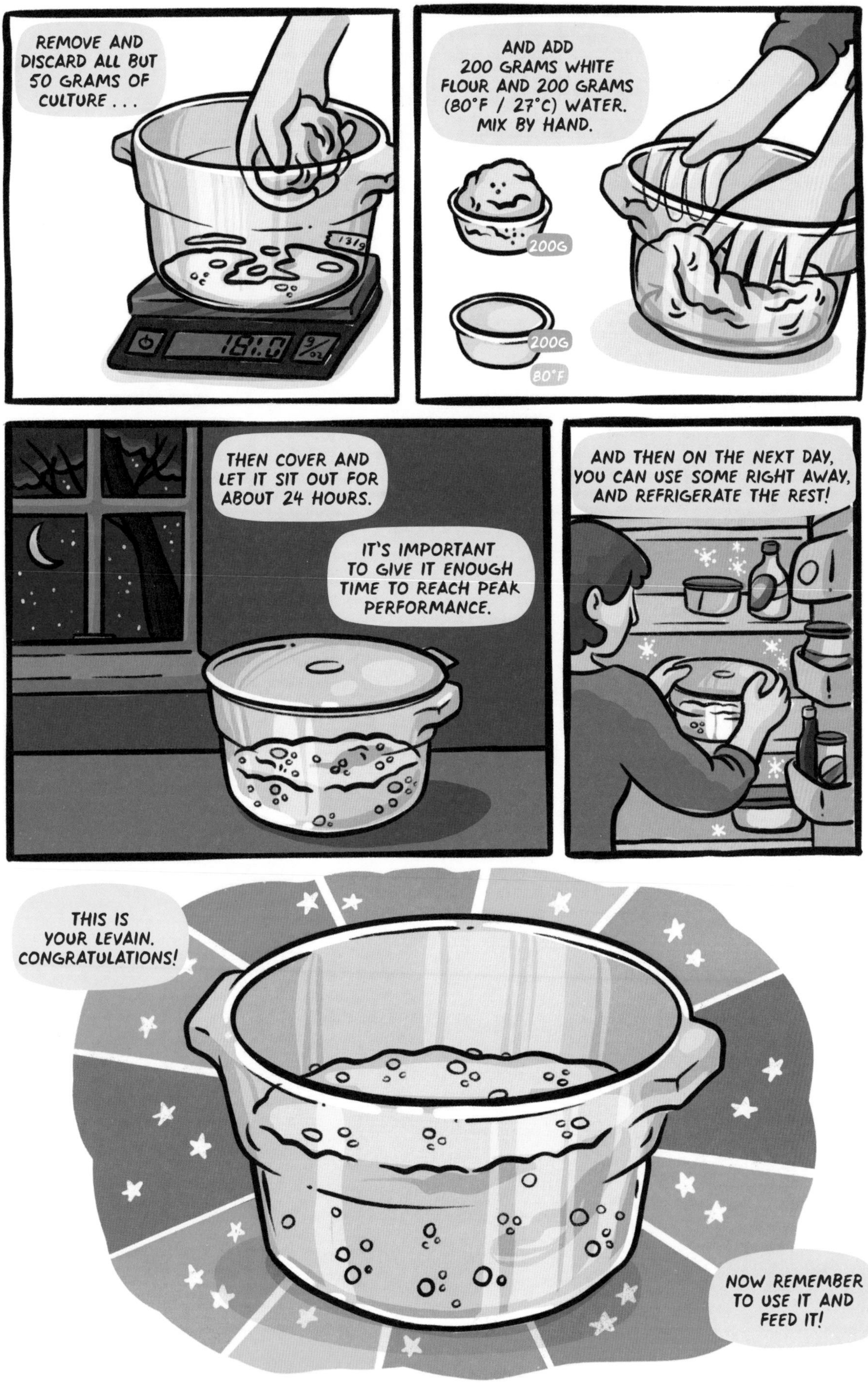
REMOVE AND DISCARD ALL BUT 50 GRAMS OF CULTURE . . .
181.0
AND ADD 200 GRAMS WHITE FLOUR AND 200 GRAMS (80°F / 27°C) WATER. MIX BY HAND.
200G
200G
80°F
THEN COVER AND LET IT SIT OUT FOR ABOUT 24 HOURS.
IT'S IMPORTANT TO GIVE IT ENOUGH TIME TO REACH PEAK PERFORMANCE.
AND THEN ON THE NEXT DAY, YOU CAN USE SOME RIGHT AWAY, AND REFRIGERATE THE REST!
THIS IS YOUR LEVAIN. CONGRATULATIONS!
NOW REMEMBER TO USE IT AND FEED IT!

MAINTENANCE FEEDINGS
EVERY 7 TO 10 DAYS (OR AS NEEDED)

EACH RECIPE IN THIS BOOK USES EITHER 50 GRAMS OR 100 GRAMS OF THIS CULTURE.

YOU'LL NEED TO FEED IT EVERY 7 TO 10 DAYS;

OR MORE OFTEN IF YOU'RE BAKING A LOT AND YOU'RE ABOUT TO RUN OUT.

WHEN IT'S TIME TO REFRESH THE CULTURE, USE THE SAME CONTAINER AS ITS PERMANENT HOME.

REMOVE ALL BUT 50 GRAMS OF WHAT IS LEFT IN THERE.

ADD 200 GRAMS WHITE FLOUR (BREAD FLOUR OR ALL-PURPOSE FLOUR IS FINE) . . .

AND 200 GRAMS WATER (75°F / 24°C IN SUMMER, 85°F / 29°C IN WINTER).

200G

200G

85°F

MIX BY HAND.

COVER AND LET IT SIT OUT AT ROOM TEMPERATURE FOR 20 TO 24 HOURS . . .

THEN REFRIGERATE.

YOUR FRESHLY FED LEVAIN IS NOW READY TO BE USED IN RECIPES AGAIN!

MORE TEMPERATURE NOTES

AGAIN, YOUR ROOM TEMPERATURE IS RELEVANT.

IF YOUR REFRESHED LEVAIN IS SITTING OUT AT, SAY, 65°F / 18°C OVERNIGHT . . .

A FULL 24 HOURS IS GOOD BEFORE REFRIGERATING IT.

BUT IF YOUR ROOM TEMPERATURE IS 80°F / 27°C . . .

YOU'LL REACH THAT SAME POINT OF MATURITY IN THE CULTURE MUCH FASTER — IN ABOUT 12 TO 16 HOURS.

NOT ENOUGH TIME WILL RESULT IN BREAD DOUGHS THAT TAKE TOO LONG TO RISE AND DON'T EVER QUITE REACH THEIR POTENTIAL VOLUME.

TOO MUCH TIME WILL OVERFERMENT THE CULTURE AND YOU'LL GET MORE SOUR FLAVORS.

KEEP BAKING, AND EVENTUALLY YOU'LL HAVE IT FIGURED OUT!

SHARE THE CULTURE

ANY TIME YOU WANT TO "GIFT" A FRESH BATCH OF LEVAIN TO A FRIEND OR FAMILY MEMBER, YOU CAN MAKE UP A NEW ONE EASILY JUST LIKE WHEN YOU REFRESH YOURS.

IN A FRESH CONTAINER, MIX 200 GRAMS (85°F / 29°C) WATER WITH 50 GRAMS OF YOUR ORIGINAL LEVAIN CULTURE.

SWISH IT AROUND WITH YOUR FINGERS...

AND THEN ADD 200 GRAMS WHITE FLOUR AND MIX BY HAND.

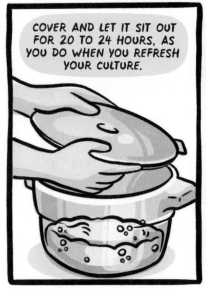

COVER AND LET IT SIT OUT FOR 20 TO 24 HOURS, AS YOU DO WHEN YOU REFRESH YOUR CULTURE.

THEN REFRIGERATE IT.

IT'S READY TO PASS ALONG!

for YOU

COLD STORAGE

WHEN YOU WON'T BE BAKING FOR A FEW WEEKS OR MORE,

YOU'LL NEED A STORAGE ROUTINE TO HOLD THE LEVAIN IN A KIND OF SUSPENSION UNTIL YOU'RE READY TO BRING IT BACK.

I'VE HELD CULTURES IN MY REFRIGERATOR FOR A COUPLE OF MONTHS AND THEN SUCCESSFULLY RESTORED THEM.

THERE ARE MANY METHODS. HERE'S WHAT WORKS FOR ME:

REMOVE 200 GRAMS OF THE LEVAIN AND PLACE IT IN A LARGE BOWL.

TOSS THE REST, AND CLEAN YOUR LEVAIN TUB FOR LATER USE.

MIX THE LEVAIN BY HAND WITH 100 GRAMS WHITE FLOUR AND 35 GRAMS COLD WATER TO FORM A STIFF DOUGH.

PUT IT INTO AN AIRTIGHT CONTAINER (LIKE A 1-QUART VESSEL WITH A MATCHING LID OR A PLASTIC BAG) . . .

AND COVER WITH ANOTHER 100 GRAMS WHITE FLOUR.

STORE IN THE REFRIGERATOR.

TO RESTORE A LEVAIN FROM COLD STORAGE

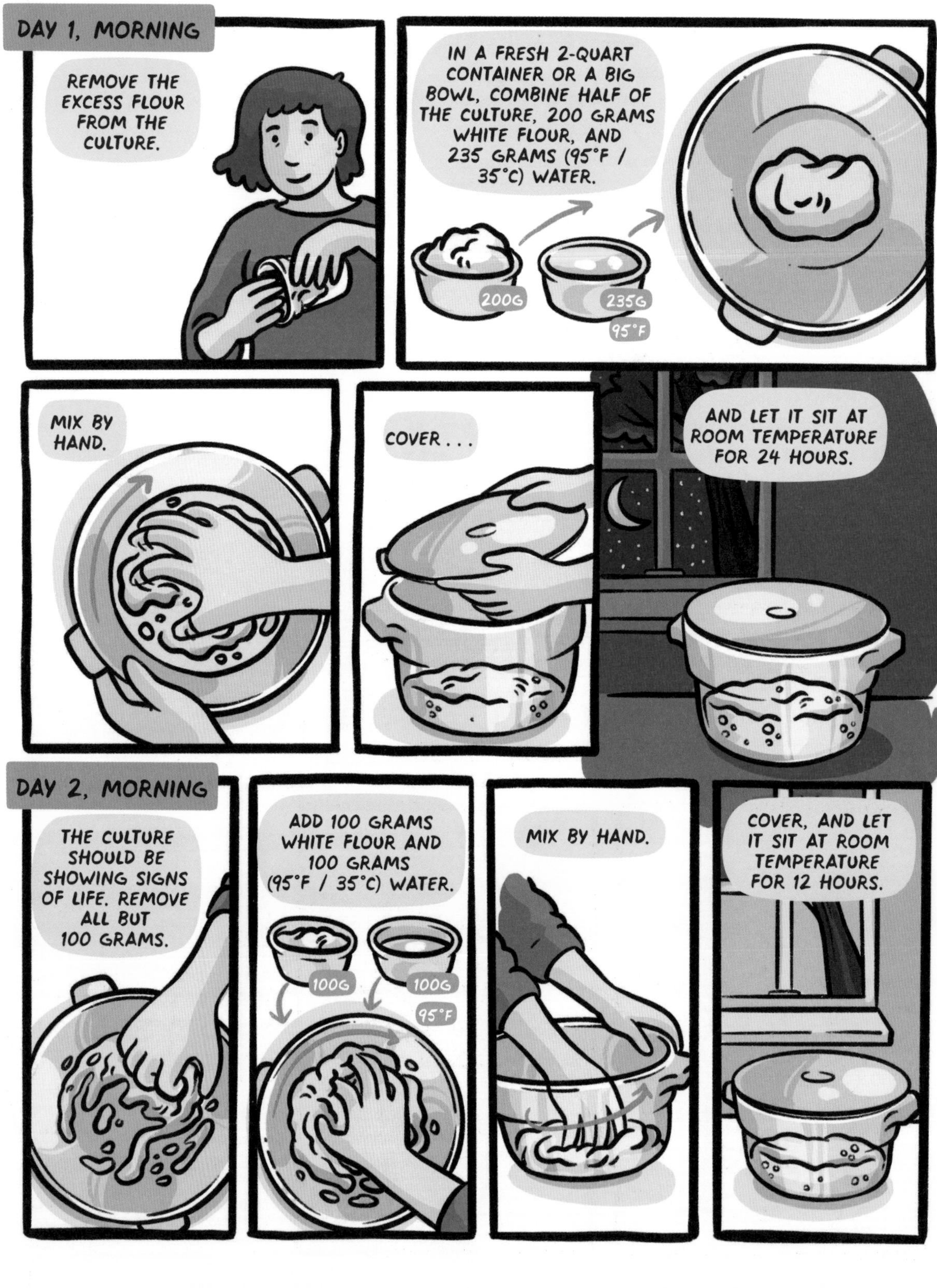
DAY 1, MORNING
REMOVE THE EXCESS FLOUR FROM THE CULTURE.
IN A FRESH 2-QUART CONTAINER OR A BIG BOWL, COMBINE HALF OF THE CULTURE, 200 GRAMS WHITE FLOUR, AND 235 GRAMS (95°F / 35°C) WATER.
200G
235G
95°F
MIX BY HAND.
COVER . . .
AND LET IT SIT AT ROOM TEMPERATURE FOR 24 HOURS.
DAY 2, MORNING
THE CULTURE SHOULD BE SHOWING SIGNS OF LIFE. REMOVE ALL BUT 100 GRAMS.
ADD 100 GRAMS WHITE FLOUR AND 100 GRAMS (95°F / 35°C) WATER.
100G
100G
95°F
MIX BY HAND.
COVER, AND LET IT SIT AT ROOM TEMPERATURE FOR 12 HOURS.

THE CULTURE SHOULD LOOK LIVELY AND FULL OF BUBBLES.

REMOVE ALL BUT 50 GRAMS . . .

AND ADD 200 GRAMS WHITE FLOUR AND 200 GRAMS (85°F / 29°C) WATER.

200G

200G

85°F

MIX BY HAND.

COVER . . .

AND LET IT SIT AT ROOM TEMPERATURE FOR 20 TO 24 HOURS.

DAY 3, EVENING

YOUR LEVAIN SHOULD NOW BE READY FOR USE.

YOU CAN RETURN IT TO THE REFRIGERATOR AND GO BACK TO YOUR WEEKLY MAINTENANCE SCHEDULE.

REPLICATION & FERMENTATION

TO HELP YOU UNDERSTAND WHAT'S GOING ON, IMAGINE WHAT'S AT WORK ON THE CELLULAR LEVEL.

YEAST CELLS DUPLICATE FAST!

ALL THEY NEED IS FOOD, WATER, OXYGEN, AND A NICE TEMPERATURE.

YEAST WILL REPLICATE AS LONG AS THERE IS OXYGEN IN THEIR ENVIRONMENT.

ONCE THE ENVIRONMENT BECOMES ANAEROBIC (WITHOUT OXYGEN), THEIR ACTIVITY CONVERTS TO FERMENTATION: THEY EAT SUGARS AND OUTPUT CO_2 GAS AND ETHANOL.

SO AFTER A CERTAIN POINT,

THE POPULATION OF YEASTS IN YOUR LEVAIN WILL SHIFT FROM MOSTLY REPLICATING TO MOSTLY FERMENTING.

BUT IT'S NOT A HARD-STOP SHIFT.

THERE'S USUALLY SOME OF EACH ACTIVITY — REPRODUCTION AND FERMENTATION — THAT'S GOING ON SIMULTANEOUSLY.

TOO MUCH FERMENTATION WILL PRODUCE ACETIC ACIDS, WHICH IS WHAT MAKES "SOURDOUGH" TASTE SOUR.

MY PROCESS AIMS TO BUILD UP A LARGE YEAST POPULATION WITHOUT GETTING TOO MUCH FERMENTATION ACTIVITY EARLY IN THE PROCESS.

THAT'S WHY WE START WITH A VERY SMALL AMOUNT OF CULTURE AND FEED IT REPEATEDLY WITH GOOD-QUALITY FLOUR AND WARM WATER.

IT'S THE BEST WAY TO GET TO MY DESIRED MELLOW LEVAIN, FULL OF FLAVORS THAT ARE COMPLEX WITHOUT BEING SOUR.

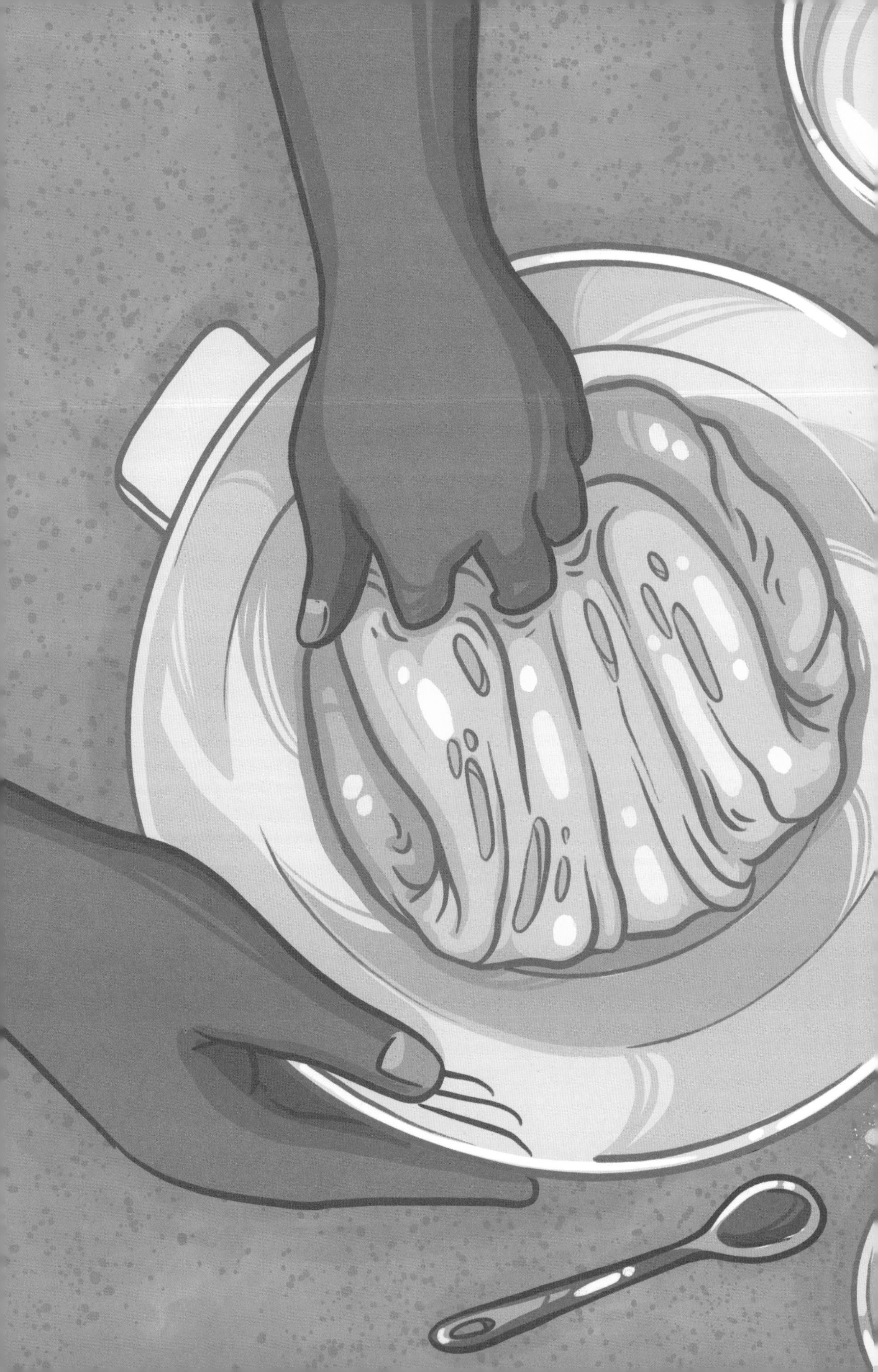

RECIPES

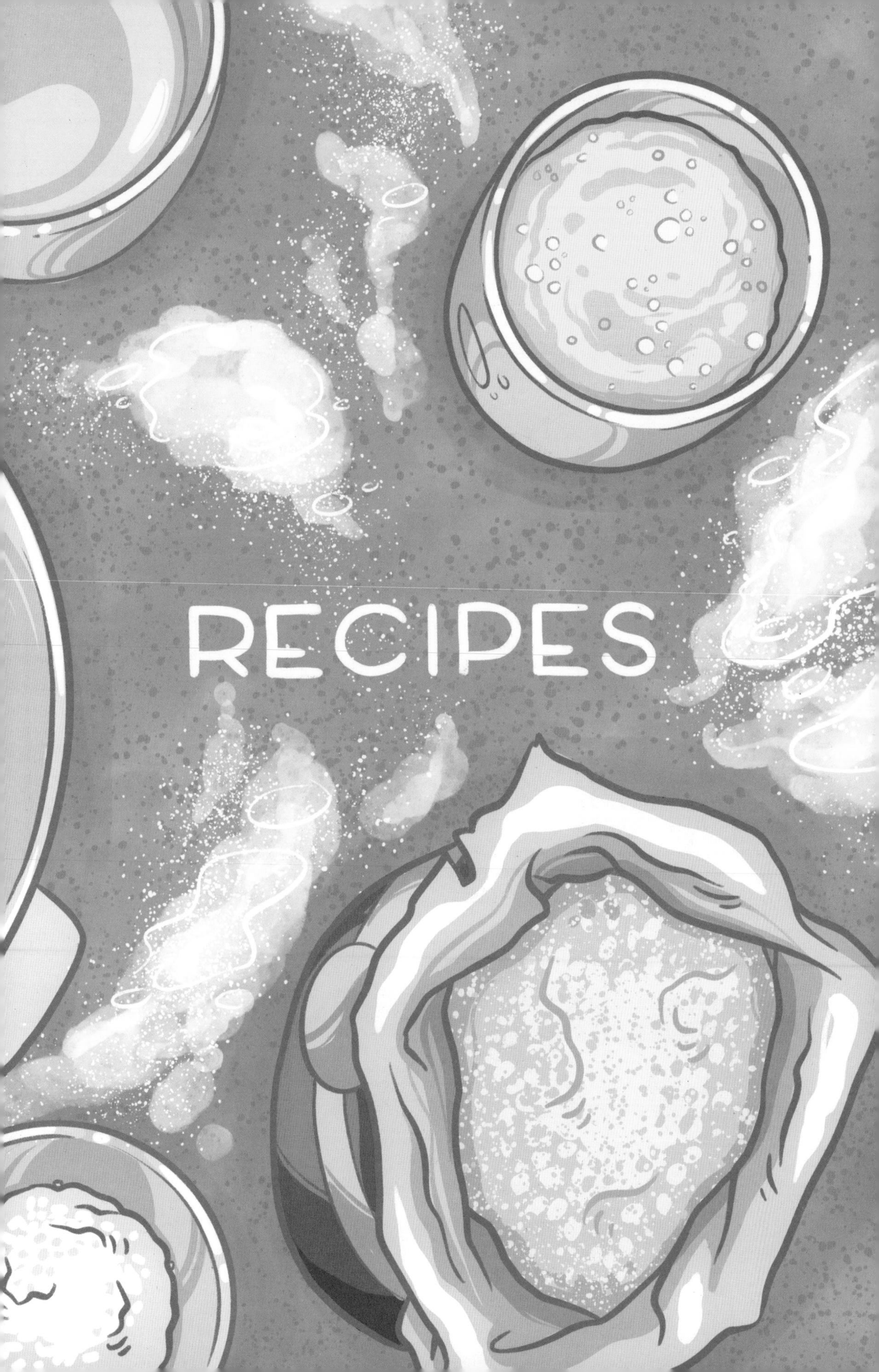

A GUIDE TO THE RECIPES

THE RECIPES THAT FOLLOW GIVE YOU A FUN RANGE OF BREADS THAT CAN BE BAKED IN A DUTCH OVEN OR A BREAD PAN.

THE FIRST RECIPE, THE SATURDAY BREAD, IS DESIGNED FOR A DUTCH OVEN, AND IT'S ADAPTED FROM *FLOUR WATER SALT YEAST* FOR A ONE-LOAF BATCH SIZE.

WE ADDED SOME RIFFS ON THE SATURDAY BREAD THAT USE THE SAME PROCESS, BUT CHANGE UP THE FLOUR BLEND OR ADD FUN STUFF TO THE DOUGH.

IT'S GREAT TO ADD SOME LEVAIN TO THESE RECIPES FOR FLAVOR (SEE PAGE 75), JUST LIMIT THE AMOUNT TO 100 GRAMS (½ CUP).

THE STANDARD AND THE MULTIGRAIN BREAD ARE SAME-DAY BREADS TOO, WITH SOURDOUGH FOR FLAVOR.

THEY WERE DESIGNED FOR OPEN BREAD PANS BUT ALSO WORK GREAT IN A DUTCH OVEN.

FOR SOURDOUGH BAKERS WE HAVE 3 PURE LEVAIN DUTCH OVEN BREAD RECIPES: COUNTRY BREAD, WALNUT BREAD, AND BACON BREAD.

THESE SOURDOUGH RECIPES HAVE YOU BUILD A STARTER FROM A REFRIGERATED LEVAIN CULTURE IN 3 STAGES, WITH NOT MUCH WASTE,

AND THE RESULTS ARE FANTASTIC!

START WITH THE SIMPLEST RECIPE, THE SATURDAY BREAD FOR DUTCH OVEN, OR THE STANDARD FOR A PAN BREAD.

SAME-DAY BREADS

	PRIMARY VESSEL	ALSO WORKS IN
THE SATURDAY BREAD (PAGE 65)	DUTCH OVEN	OPEN PAN

RIFFS ON THE SATURDAY BREAD:

40% WHOLE-WHEAT BREAD (PAGE 77)	DUTCH OVEN	OPEN PAN
CORN KERNEL BREAD (PAGE 78)	OPEN PAN	DUTCH OVEN
BUTTER BREAD (PAGE 79)	OPEN PAN	DUTCH OVEN
RAISIN-PECAN BREAD (PAGE 82)	DUTCH OVEN	OPEN PAN

THE STANDARD (PAGE 85)	OPEN PAN	DUTCH OVEN

A RIFF ON THE STANDARD:

THE STANDARD #2 (PAGE 96)	OPEN PAN	DUTCH OVEN

MULTIGRAIN BREAD (PAGE 102)	OPEN PAN	DUTCH OVEN

DUTCH OVEN LEVAIN BREADS

COUNTRY BREAD (PAGE 114)	DUTCH OVEN	

A RIFF ON THE COUNTRY BREAD:

WALNUT BREAD (PAGE 127)	DUTCH OVEN	

BACON BREAD (PAGE 128)	DUTCH OVEN	

BAKER'S MATH

BAKER'S MATH IS A SIMPLE WAY TO UNDERSTAND A RECIPE.

THE TOTAL AMOUNT OF FLOURS IN THE DOUGH IS ALWAYS TREATED AS 100%...

AND EACH INGREDIENT IS VIEWED AS A PERCENTAGE OF THE TOTAL WEIGHT OF FLOUR.

FOR EXAMPLE: DIVIDE THE AMOUNT OF WATER BY THE AMOUNT OF FLOUR.

360 GRAMS OF WATER IN A RECIPE WITH 500 GRAMS FLOUR = 72% WATER!

$$\frac{360 \div 500}{72}$$

WE INCLUDE THE BAKER'S PERCENTAGES IN THE CHARTS AT THE BEGINNING OF EACH RECIPE.

YOU CAN RELIABLY WORK ANY RECIPE JUST BY KNOWING THE PERCENTAGES.

LIKE THIS FOR THE SATURDAY BREAD:

FLOUR IS 500 GRAMS = 100%
WATER IS 360 GRAMS = 72%
SALT IS 11 GRAMS = 2.2%
YEAST IS 2 GRAMS = 0.4%

FLOUR 100%
WATER 72%
SALT 2.2%
YEAST .4%

THE SATURDAY BREAD

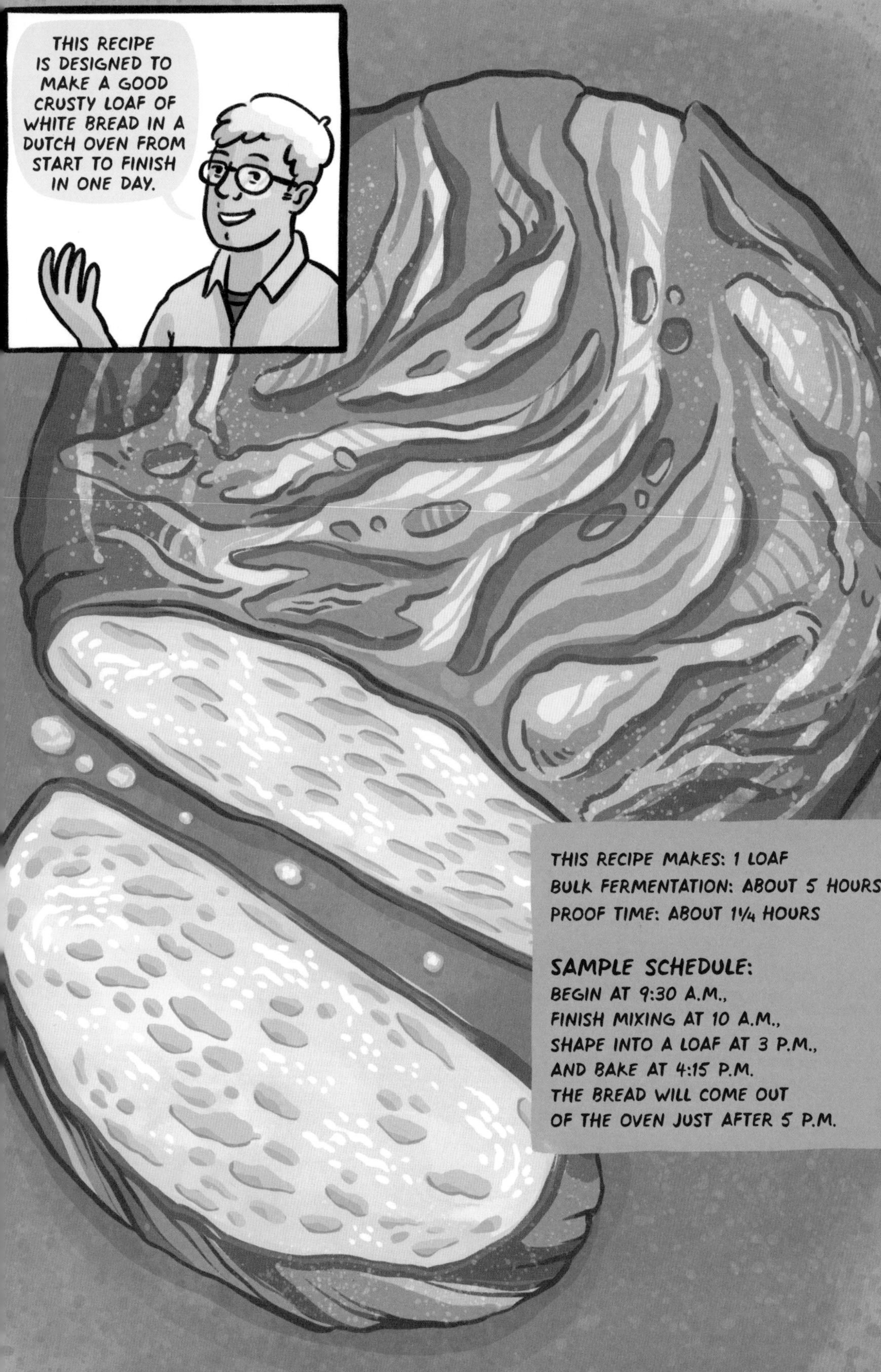
THIS RECIPE IS DESIGNED TO MAKE A GOOD CRUSTY LOAF OF WHITE BREAD IN A DUTCH OVEN FROM START TO FINISH IN ONE DAY.

THIS RECIPE MAKES: 1 LOAF
BULK FERMENTATION: ABOUT 5 HOURS
PROOF TIME: ABOUT 1¼ HOURS

SAMPLE SCHEDULE:
BEGIN AT 9:30 A.M.,
FINISH MIXING AT 10 A.M.,
SHAPE INTO A LOAF AT 3 P.M.,
AND BAKE AT 4:15 P.M.
THE BREAD WILL COME OUT
OF THE OVEN JUST AFTER 5 P.M.

INGREDIENT	QUANTITY		BAKER'S %
WHITE BREAD FLOUR	500G	3 ½ CUPS + 1 TBSP + 1 TSP	100%
WATER	360G 90° TO 95°F / 32° TO 35°C	1 ½ CUPS + SCANT 2 TSP	72%
FINE SEA SALT	11G	2 ¼ TSP	2.2%
INSTANT DRIED YEAST	2G	½ TSP	0.4%

1: AUTOLYSE

COMBINE 500 GRAMS FLOUR WITH 360 GRAMS (90° TO 95°F / 32° TO 35°C) WATER IN A 6-QUART ROUND TUB OR SIMILAR CONTAINER.

MIX BY HAND JUST UNTIL INCORPORATED.

COVER AND LET REST FOR 15 TO 20 MINUTES.

2: MIX

SPRINKLE 11 GRAMS SALT AND 2 GRAMS (½ TEASPOON) YEAST EVENLY OVER THE TOP OF THE DOUGH.

MIX BY HAND, WETTING YOUR WORKING HAND BEFORE MIXING SO THE DOUGH DOESN'T STICK TO YOU.

(IT'S FINE TO REWET YOUR HAND 3 OR 4 TIMES WHILE YOU MIX.)

REACH UNDERNEATH THE DOUGH AND GRAB ABOUT ONE-FOURTH OF IT.

GENTLY STRETCH THIS SECTION OF DOUGH . . .

AND FOLD IT OVER THE TOP TO THE OTHER SIDE OF THE DOUGH.

REPEAT 3 MORE TIMES WITH THE REMAINING DOUGH, UNTIL THE SALT AND YEAST ARE FULLY ENCLOSED.

USE THE PINCER METHOD (PAGE 30) TO FULLY INTEGRATE THE INGREDIENTS.

MAKE 5 OR 6 PINCER CUTS ACROSS THE ENTIRE MASS OF DOUGH.

THEN FOLD THE DOUGH OVER ITSELF A FEW TIMES.

REPEAT, ALTERNATELY CUTTING AND FOLDING, UNTIL ALL OF THE INGREDIENTS ARE FULLY INTEGRATED AND THE DOUGH HAS SOME TENSION IN IT.

LET THE DOUGH REST FOR A FEW MINUTES . . .

THEN FOLD FOR ANOTHER 30 SECONDS OR UNTIL THE DOUGH TIGHTENS UP.

THE WHOLE PROCESS SHOULD TAKE ABOUT 5 MINUTES. THE TARGET DOUGH TEMPERATURE AT THE END OF THE MIX IS 77° TO 78°F / 25° TO 26°C.

COVER THE TUB AND LET THE DOUGH RISE.

3: FOLD & FIRST RISE

THIS DOUGH NEEDS 2 FOLDS (SEE PAGE 31 FOR INSTRUCTIONS).

IT'S EASIEST TO APPLY THE FOLDS DURING THE FIRST HOUR AFTER MIXING THE DOUGH.

APPLY THE FIRST FOLD ABOUT 10 MINUTES AFTER MIXING . . .

AND APPLY THE SECOND FOLD ANYTIME DURING THE NEXT HOUR.

WHEN YOU SEE THE DOUGH SPREAD OUT IN THE TUB, IT'S READY FOR THE SECOND FOLD.

IF NEED BE, IT'S OKAY TO FOLD LATER; JUST BE SURE TO LEAVE IT ALONE FOR THE LAST HOUR OF RISING.

WHEN THE DOUGH IS ABOUT 2 ½ TIMES ITS ORIGINAL VOLUME, ABOUT 5 HOURS AFTER MIXING, IT'S READY TO BE MADE UP INTO A LOAF.

IT SHOULD HAVE RISEN TO JUST SHY OF THE 2-QUART LINE (ABOUT ¼ INCH) IN A 6-QUART DOUGH TUB.

USE THAT AMOUNT OF RISE AS YOUR ULTIMATE GUIDE FOR WHEN IT'S READY FOR THE NEXT STEP.

LIGHTLY FLOUR A WORK SURFACE ABOUT 12 INCHES WIDE.

FLOUR YOUR HANDS...

AND SPRINKLE A BIT OF FLOUR AROUND THE EDGES OF THE TUB.

TIP THE TUB SLIGHTLY...

AND THEN GENTLY WORK YOUR FLOURED FREE HAND BENEATH THE DOUGH TO LOOSEN IT FROM THE BOTTOM OF THE TUB.

THEN TURN THE TUB ON ITS SIDE...

AND EASE THE DOUGH ONTO THE WORK SURFACE WITHOUT PULLING OR TEARING IT.

5: SHAPE

DUST A PROOFING BASKET MODERATELY WITH FLOUR.

USE ENOUGH FLOUR SO THE FULLY PROOFED LOAF CAN BE REMOVED WITHOUT STICKING, BUT NOT SO MUCH THAT YOU HAVE A LOT OF EXCESS FLOUR ON THE LOAF.

SHAPE THE DOUGH INTO A MEDIUM-TIGHT BALL FOLLOWING THE INSTRUCTIONS ON PAGE 34.

PLACE YOUR SHAPED LOAF SEAM SIDE DOWN IN THE FLOURED PROOFING BASKET.

6: PROOF

PLACE THE BASKET IN A PLASTIC BAG TO KEEP IT FROM DRYING OUT.

IT DOESN'T HAVE TO BE AIRTIGHT.

IF YOUR ROOM TEMPERATURE IS ABOUT 70°F / 21°C, PLAN ON BAKING THE LOAF ABOUT 1¼ HOURS AFTER IT IS SHAPED.

IF YOUR KITCHEN IS WARMER, IT WILL BE OPTIMALLY PROOFED IN ABOUT 1 HOUR.

USE THE FINGER-DENT TEST (SEE PAGE 36) TO DETERMINE WHEN IT'S PERFECTLY PROOFED AND READY TO BAKE!

NO MATTER YOUR ROOM TEMPERATURE, CHECK ON IT AFTER AN HOUR TO SEE IF IT'S PROOFED.

WITH THIS LOAF, 15 MINUTES CAN MAKE THE DIFFERENCE BETWEEN BEING PERFECTLY PROOFED AND COLLAPSING A BIT.

AT LEAST 45 MINUTES PRIOR TO BAKING, PUT A RACK IN THE MIDDLE OF THE OVEN.

AND PUT YOUR DUTCH OVEN ON THE RACK WITH ITS LID ON.

PREHEAT THE OVEN TO 475°F / 245°C.

INVERT THE PROOFED LOAF ONTO A LIGHTLY FLOURED COUNTERTOP.

THE TOP OF THE LOAF WILL BE THE SIDE THAT WAS FACING DOWN WHILE IT WAS RISING— THE SEAM SIDE.

FOR THIS NEXT STEP, PLEASE BE CAREFUL NOT TO LET YOUR HANDS, FINGERS, OR FOREARMS TOUCH THE EXTREMELY HOT DUTCH OVEN!

USE OVEN MITTS TO REMOVE THE PREHEATED DUTCH OVEN FROM THE OVEN.

REMOVE THE LID.

CAREFULLY PLACE THE LOAF IN THE HOT DUTCH OVEN SEAM SIDE UP.

USE MITTS TO REPLACE THE LID . . .

THEN PUT THE DUTCH OVEN BACK IN THE OVEN.

BAKE FOR 30 MINUTES.

THEN CAREFULLY REMOVE THE LID AND BAKE FOR ABOUT 20 MINUTES MORE . . .

UNTIL AT LEAST MEDIUM DARK BROWN ALL AROUND THE LOAF.

CHECK AFTER 15 MINUTES OF BAKING UNCOVERED IN CASE YOUR OVEN RUNS HOT.

REMOVE THE DUTCH OVEN . . .

AND CAREFULLY TILT IT TO TURN THE LOAF OUT.

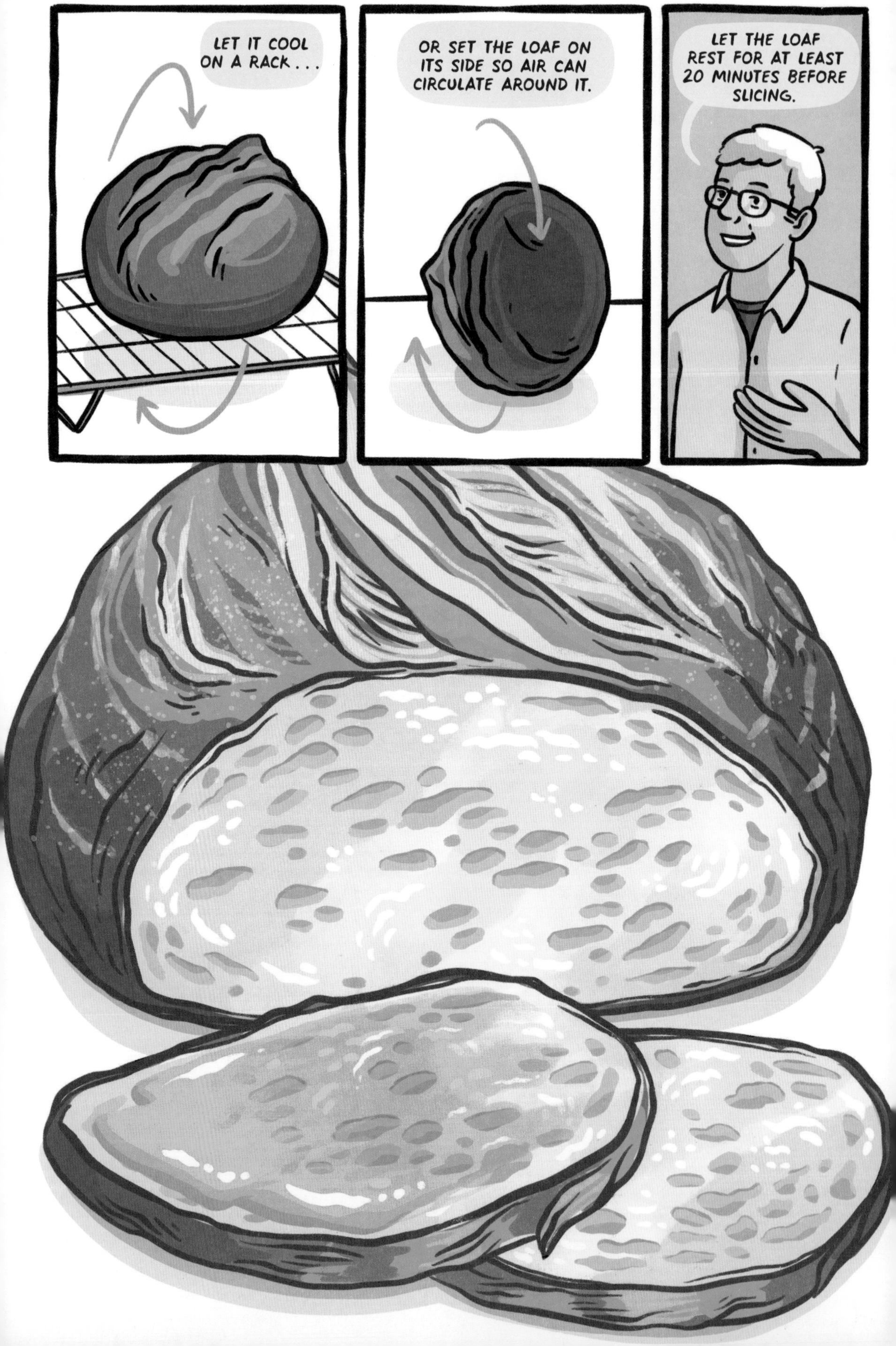
LET IT COOL ON A RACK . . .
OR SET THE LOAF ON ITS SIDE SO AIR CAN CIRCULATE AROUND IT.
LET THE LOAF REST FOR AT LEAST 20 MINUTES BEFORE SLICING.

ADDING LEVAIN TO SAME-DAY BREADS

DO YOU WANT TO ADD SOME OF THIS BOOK'S REFRIGERATED LEVAIN TO THE SATURDAY BREAD?

IT'S EASY AND DELICIOUS!

SECRET SAUCE!

AFTER YOU MEASURE WATER INTO YOUR DOUGH TUB (OR WATER AND TEA FOR THE RAISIN-PECAN BREAD) . . .

ADD TO IT 100 GRAMS OF THE LEVAIN THAT YOU HAVE MADE UP.

STIR IT UP WITH YOUR WORKING HAND.

THEN ADD THE OTHER INGREDIENTS AND FOLLOW THE REST OF THE RECIPE AS WRITTEN.

RIFFS ON THE SATURDAY BREAD

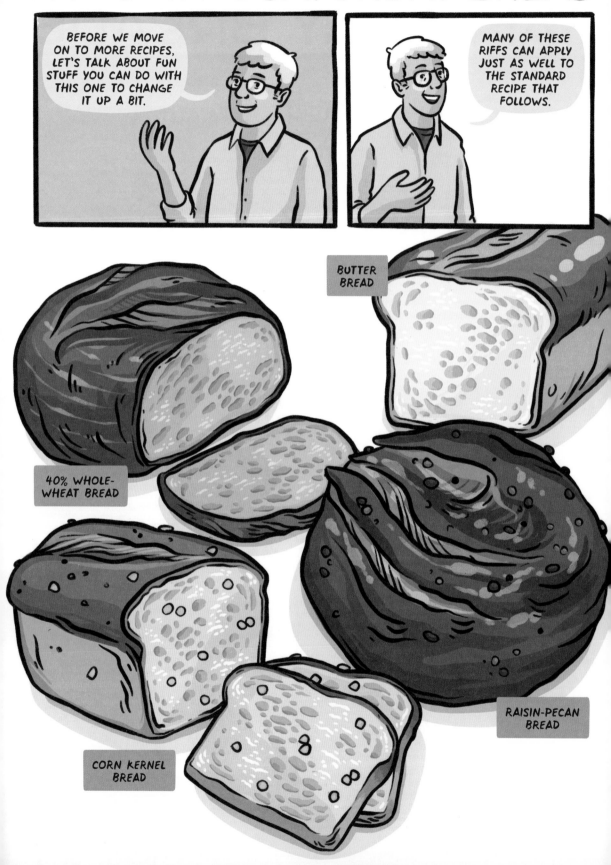

40% WHOLE-WHEAT BREAD

LET'S MAKE A 40% WHOLE-WHEAT BREAD USING THE SATURDAY BREAD AS THE MODEL.

YOU CAN CHANGE THE FLOUR BLEND, ESPECIALLY IF YOU HAVE SOME GOOD STONE-MILLED HERITAGE WHEAT FLOUR.

YOU'LL USE THE SAME AMOUNT OF TOTAL FLOUR IN THE RECIPE, 500 GRAMS.

300G WHITE BREAD FLOUR

200G WHOLE-WHEAT FLOUR

500G TOTAL FLOUR

WHOLE-GRAIN FLOUR IS MORE ABSORBENT THAN WHITE FLOUR, SO WE PUT MORE WATER IN THE DOUGH.

SO, FOR EXAMPLE:

300 GRAMS WHITE BREAD FLOUR

200 GRAMS WHOLE-WHEAT FLOUR

11 GRAMS SALT AND 2 GRAMS YEAST

400 GRAMS WATER

FOLLOW THE REST OF THE DIRECTIONS FOR THE SATURDAY BREAD!

FOR A LITTLE MORE FUN, LET'S TRY ADDING STUFF TO THE DOUGH.

CORN KERNEL BREAD

MEASURE OUT 150 GRAMS OF FRESH-CUT CORN KERNELS.

THIS WORKS OUT TO BE ABOUT 1 EAR, MAYBE 2 EARS DEPENDING ON SIZE.

OR ABOUT 1 TO 1½ CUPS OF CORN KERNELS.

IN THE AUTOLYSE STEP FOR THE SATURDAY BREAD DOUGH (OR THE STANDARD DOUGH) . . .

ADD THE CORN KERNELS TO THE WATER, AND MIX IT UP WITH THE FLOUR.

FOLLOW ALL THE REST OF THE STEPS IN THE BASE RECIPE . . .

TO MAKE A DELICIOUS LOAF STUDDED WITH SWEET FRESH CORN!

BUTTER BREAD

THIS ONE REQUIRES A STAND MIXER AND A DOUGH HOOK ATTACHMENT!

MIX THE SATURDAY DOUGH BY HAND, THROUGH STEP 2 OF THE BASE RECIPE.

OR TRY THIS WITH THE STANDARD DOUGH!

MEASURE 100 GRAMS COLD BUTTER ON YOUR SCALE.

USE A KNIFE OR BAKER'S BENCH SCRAPER TO CUT THE BUTTER INTO ABOUT A DOZEN CHUNKS THE SIZE OF GRAPES.

TOSS THE BUTTER IN ABOUT A TABLESPOON OF FLOUR FOR "GRIP."

PUT THE MIXED DOUGH INTO THE STAND MIXER'S BOWL . . .

AND SCATTER THE BUTTER PIECES ON TOP OF THE DOUGH.

MIX ON LOW SPEED FOR ABOUT 2 MINUTES . . .

AND THEN MIX ON MEDIUM-HIGH SPEED FOR ABOUT 5 MINUTES MORE.

WHEN YOU DON'T SEE ANY MORE BUTTER CHUNKS, AND IT'S ALL BLENDED INTO THE DOUGH, IT'S READY!

REMOVE THE DOUGH FROM THE MIXER BOWL AND FOLD IT ON A LIGHTLY FLOURED SURFACE.

THEN PUT IT INTO YOUR DOUGH TUB, COVER, AND LET IT RISE.

APPLY 1 OR 2 MORE FOLDS DURING THE FIRST HOUR OF THE RISE.

LET THE DOUGH RISE UNTIL IT'S ABOUT 2 ½ TIMES ITS ORIGINAL VOLUME.

THE AMOUNT OF TIME THIS TAKES WILL DEPEND ON WHICH RECIPE YOU BASED IT ON.

THE SATURDAY BREAD TAKES LONGER TO RISE THAN THE STANDARD.

KEEP AN EYE ON IT, BECAUSE IT WILL RISE FASTER THAN THE OTHER DOUGHS!

TRANSFER THE DOUGH, IN ITS TUB, TO THE FRIDGE FOR THE LAST HOUR OF ITS RISE.

THE DOUGH SHOULD RISE UP TO ABOUT THE 2-QUART LINE ON THE DOUGH TUB.

REMOVE THE DOUGH FROM THE TUB AND SHAPE INTO A LOAF WHILE IT'S STILL COLD . . .

THEN PROOF THE DOUGH FOR ABOUT 1 HOUR.

FOR A DUTCH OVEN LOAF, BAKE AT THE SAME TIME AND TEMPERATURE AS THE SATURDAY BREAD.

OR, IF YOU MAKE IT INTO A PAN LOAF, BAKE AT 425°F / 220°C FOR 50 MINUTES.

RAISIN-PECAN BREAD

THIS MAKES A GREAT DUTCH OVEN LOAF OR PAN BREAD!

SOMETIMES I LIKE TO USE A LITTLE BIT OF DARK OR WHOLE RYE FLOUR IN THE DOUGH MIX (10% TO 15% OF THE TOTAL FLOUR IS GOOD).

JUST KEEP THE TOTAL AMOUNT OF FLOUR THE SAME AS IN THE BASE RECIPE.

FOR EXAMPLE:

375 GRAMS WHITE BREAD FLOUR

50 GRAMS WHOLE-WHEAT FLOUR

75 GRAMS RYE FLOUR

370 GRAMS LIQUID (WATER PLUS TEA, IN THIS RECIPE)

11 GRAMS SALT AND 2 GRAMS YEAST

START BY BREWING ABOUT 1½ CUPS OF EARL GREY TEA.

ADD 100 GRAMS RAISINS TO SOAK.

I LIKE TO BLEND YELLOW AND PURPLE RAISINS.

SOAK THE RAISINS FOR A COUPLE OF HOURS, OR OVERNIGHT IF YOU CAN.

YOU WANT ENOUGH TIME FOR THE LIQUID TO RETURN TO ROOM TEMPERATURE...

AND FOR THE RAISINS TO HAVE FULLY ABSORBED THE TEA.

FOR THE AUTOLYSE STEP OF YOUR BREAD RECIPE, STRAIN THE RAISINS, RESERVING THE SOAKING LIQUID.

SQUEEZE OUT THE EXCESS LIQUID FROM THE RAISINS.

MEASURE 185 GRAMS OF THE SOAKING LIQUID INTO YOUR DOUGH TUB.

ADD 185 GRAMS (90° TO 95°F / 32° TO 35°C) WATER TO BRING THE TOTAL LIQUID TO 370 GRAMS.

ADD THE RAISINS TO THE DOUGH TUB.

ADD 100 GRAMS OF THE OPTIONAL LEVAIN IF YOU ARE USING IT, AND MIX IT INTO THE LIQUID WITH YOUR FINGERS.

ADD THE FLOURS TO THE DOUGH TUB . . .

THEN MEASURE 80 TO 100 GRAMS PECAN PIECES AND ADD TO THE TUB.

MIX BY HAND. REST THE DOUGH FOR 15 MINUTES, ADD THE SALT AND YEAST, AND FOLLOW THE REST OF YOUR RECIPE STEPS.

KEEP AN EYE ON IT DURING THE RISE! THIS DOUGH WILL RISE FASTER THAN USUAL.

THE STANDARD

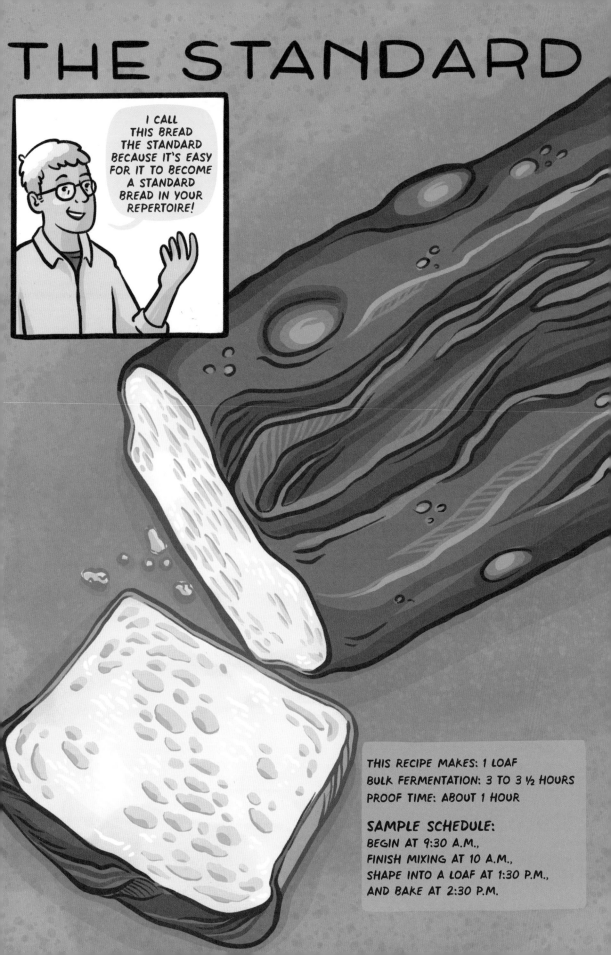

THIS RECIPE MAKES: 1 LOAF
BULK FERMENTATION: 3 TO 3 ½ HOURS
PROOF TIME: ABOUT 1 HOUR

SAMPLE SCHEDULE:
BEGIN AT 9:30 A.M.,
FINISH MIXING AT 10 A.M.,
SHAPE INTO A LOAF AT 1:30 P.M.,
AND BAKE AT 2:30 P.M.

THIS IS MY GO-TO MORNING TOAST BREAD, AND IT WORKS FOR ANY SANDWICH, CROUTONS, A CHEESY FRENCH TOAST, AND MORE.

THIS BREAD ISN'T FLASHY, BUT IT'S EASY TO EXECUTE, TASTES GREAT, AND LASTS FOR ABOUT 5 DAYS WITHOUT GOING STALE.

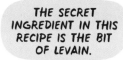

THE SECRET INGREDIENT IN THIS RECIPE IS THE BIT OF LEVAIN.

YOU CAN MAKE THIS BREAD WITHOUT IT, BUT YOU WILL BE REWARDED IF YOU INCLUDE IT.

INGREDIENT	QUANTITY		BAKER'S %
WHITE FLOUR	400G	2 ¾ CUPS + 2 TSP	80%
WHOLE-WHEAT FLOUR	100G	⅔ CUP + 1 TBSP + 1 ¼ TSP	20%
WATER	390G 90° TO 95°F / 32° TO 35°C	1 ½ CUPS + 2 TBSP	78%
FINE SEA SALT	11G	2 ¼ TSP	2.2%
INSTANT DRIED YEAST	3G	3/4 TSP	0.6%
LEVAIN (OPTIONAL)	100G	1/2 CUP	9% OF TOTAL FLOUR

1: AUTOLYSE

MEASURE 390 GRAMS (90° TO 95°F / 32° TO 35°) WATER INTO A 6-QUART ROUND TUB OR SIMILAR CONTAINER.

IF YOU HAVE A LEVAIN, ADD 100 GRAMS FROM THE REFRIGERATOR.

YOU CAN WEIGH IT DIRECTLY INTO THE DOUGH TUB WITH ITS WATER.

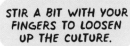

STIR A BIT WITH YOUR FINGERS TO LOOSEN UP THE CULTURE.

ADD 400 GRAMS WHITE BREAD FLOUR AND 100 GRAMS WHOLE-WHEAT FLOUR.

MIX IT BY HAND UNTIL ALL IS INCORPORATED.

SPRINKLE 11 GRAMS FINE SEA SALT AND 3 GRAMS INSTANT DRIED YEAST EVENLY ACROSS THE TOP OF THE AUTOLYSE DOUGH.

LET THEM REST THERE, WHERE THEY WILL PARTIALLY DISSOLVE.

COVER AND LET REST FOR 15 TO 20 MINUTES.

MIX BY HAND, WETTING YOUR WORKING HAND BEFORE MIXING SO THE DOUGH DOESN'T STICK TO YOU.

REACH UNDERNEATH THE DOUGH AND GRAB ABOUT ONE-FOURTH OF IT.

GENTLY STRETCH THIS SECTION AND FOLD IT OVER THE TOP TO THE OTHER SIDE OF THE DOUGH.

REPEAT 3 MORE TIMES WITH THE REMAINING DOUGH UNTIL THE SALT AND YEAST ARE FULLY ENCLOSED.

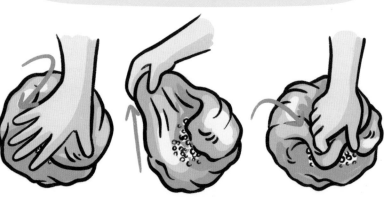

USE THE PINCER METHOD TO FULLY INTEGRATE THE INGREDIENTS.

MAKE 5 OR 6 PINCER CUTS ACROSS THE ENTIRE MASS OF DOUGH.

THEN FOLD THE DOUGH OVER ITSELF A FEW TIMES.

REPEAT, ALTERNATELY CUTTING AND FOLDING, UNTIL ALL THE INGREDIENTS ARE FULLY INTEGRATED.

LET THE DOUGH REST FOR A FEW MINUTES . . .

THEN FOLD FOR ANOTHER 30 SECONDS OR UNTIL THE DOUGH TIGHTENS UP. THE WHOLE PROCESS SHOULD TAKE ABOUT 5 MINUTES.

THE TARGET DOUGH TEMPERATURE AT THE END OF THE MIX IS ABOUT 75°F / 24°C.

COVER THE TUB AND LET THE DOUGH RISE UNTIL THE NEXT FOLD.

3: FOLD & FIRST RISE

THIS DOUGH NEEDS 2 FOLDS.

APPLY THE FOLDS DURING THE FIRST HOUR AFTER MIXING THE DOUGH.

APPLY THE FIRST FOLD ABOUT 10 MINUTES AFTER MIXING . . .

AND THE SECOND WHEN YOU SEE THE DOUGH SPREAD OUT IN THE TUB.

IF NEED BE, IT'S OKAY TO FOLD LATER; JUST BE SURE TO LEAVE IT ALONE FOR THE LAST HOUR OF RISING.

WHEN THE DOUGH IS 2½ TO 3 TIMES ITS ORIGINAL VOLUME, 3 TO 3½ HOURS AFTER THE MIX,

IT'S READY TO BE MADE UP INTO A LOAF AND PUT INTO ITS PAN.

IF YOU ARE USING A 6-QUART DOUGH TUB, THE IDEAL POINT IS WHEN THE EDGE OF THE DOUGH HAS REACHED JUST SHY (ABOUT ¼ INCH) OF THE 2-QUART LINE.

THE DOUGH WILL BE DOMED – NOT FLATTENED, NOT COLLAPSED.

IF IT REACHES THE 2-QUART LINE ON YOUR DOUGH TUB, THAT'S FINE TOO, BUT DON'T LET IT GO BEYOND THAT.

IF THE ROOM IS COOL AND THE DOUGH IS TAKING LONGER, LET IT CONTINUE TO RISE UNTIL IT REACHES THIS AMOUNT OF VOLUME EXPANSION.

IF YOU'RE NOT USING A MARKED DOUGH TUB, YOU'LL HAVE TO EYEBALL IT. USE YOUR BEST JUDGMENT.

LIGHTLY FLOUR A WORK SURFACE ABOUT 12 INCHES WIDE.

FLOUR YOUR HANDS . . .

AND SPRINKLE A BIT OF FLOUR AROUND THE EDGES OF THE TUB.

TIP THE TUB SLIGHTLY . . .

AND THEN GENTLY WORK YOUR FLOURED FREE HAND BENEATH THE DOUGH TO LOOSEN IT FROM THE BOTTOM OF THE TUB.

THEN TURN THE TUB ON ITS SIDE . . .

AND EASE THE DOUGH ONTO THE WORK SURFACE WITHOUT PULLING OR TEARING IT.

EVEN IF YOUR BREAD PAN IS NONSTICK, I HIGHLY RECOMMEND GIVING IT A LIGHT SPRITZ OF COOKING SPRAY.

NONSTICK PANS ARE SOMETIMES NOT 100 PERCENT NONSTICK IF THEY HAVE BEEN USED A LOT.

WITH FLOURED HANDS, PICK UP THE DOUGH AND EASE IT BACK ONTO THE WORK SURFACE IN A SOMEWHAT EVEN, RECTANGULAR SHAPE.

STRETCH THE DOUGH, SIMULTANEOUSLY PULLING IT RIGHT AND LEFT UNTIL IT RESISTS.

AND THEN FOLD THE ENDS BACK OVER EACH OTHER, CREATING A "PACKET" THE WIDTH OF YOUR BAKING PAN.

BRUSH OFF ANY LOOSE FLOUR FROM THE TOP OF THE DOUGH . . .

AND DO A ROLL-UP MOTION FROM THE BOTTOM UP OR FROM TOP TO BOTTOM . . .

TO FORM A TUBE OF DOUGH THAT'S ABOUT THE SAME WIDTH AS YOUR BAKING PAN.

PLACE THE DOUGH SEAM SIDE UP INTO THE PAN.

DON'T STRESS THIS PART! THE PAN DOES MUCH OF THE WORK FOR YOU.

EVEN IF ALL YOU CAN MANAGE IS TO GET THE DOUGH INTO THE PAN, IT'LL WORK FINE.

6: PROOF

USE YOUR HAND TO APPLY A LIGHT FILM OF WATER ACROSS THE ENTIRE TOP SURFACE OF THE DOUGH.

PLACE YOUR BREAD PAN IN A PLASTIC BAG.

LEAVE A FEW INCHES OF ROOM AT THE TOP FOR THE DOUGH TO EXPAND, AND TUCK THE BAG UNDER THE PAN.

IT DOESN'T NEED TO BE AIRTIGHT. THE POINT OF THE BAG IS TO KEEP THE DOUGH FROM DRYING OUT DURING THE NEXT HOUR OF PROOF TIME.

WITH MY USUAL BREAD PAN (8 ½" BY 4 ½" BY 2 ¾"), I LIKE TO SEE THE DOUGH RISING A BIT ABOVE THE RIM OF THE PAN BEFORE BAKING.

IF YOUR PAN IS LARGER, THE DOUGH LIKELY WON'T RISE ABOVE ITS RIM.

IF YOUR ROOM TEMPERATURE IS ABOUT 70°F / 21°C, PLAN ON BAKING THE LOAF ABOUT AN HOUR AFTER IT IS SHAPED.

IF YOUR KITCHEN IS WARMER, IT WILL BE OPTIMALLY PROOFED EARLIER.

7: PREHEAT

ABOUT 45 MINUTES PRIOR TO BAKING, POSITION A RACK IN THE MIDDLE OF THE OVEN . . .

AND PREHEAT THE OVEN TO 450°F / 230°C.

8: BAKE

REMOVE THE PAN FROM THE PLASTIC BAG...

AND PLACE IT ON THE CENTER OF THE MIDDLE RACK.

TURN DOWN THE HEAT TO 425°F / 220°C AND BAKE.

AFTER 30 MINUTES, CHECK THAT IT'S BAKING EVENLY.

IF IT'S NOT, GIVE THE PAN A TURN...

AND BAKE FOR ANOTHER 20 MINUTES.

THIS DOUGH HAS MORE WATER THAN TRADITIONAL PAN LOAVES,

SO IT NEEDS A LONGER TIME THAN YOU MIGHT THINK TO BAKE THE INSIDE FULLY,

AND TO GIVE THE SIDES ENOUGH STRENGTH TO AVOID POST-BAKE COLLAPSE.

AFTER 50 MINUTES, THE TOP OF THE LOAF SHOULD BE DARKLY COLORED. THE SIDES AND BOTTOM SHOULD BE GOLDEN, NOT AS DARK AS THE TOP.

REMOVE THE PAN WITH OVEN MITTS OR THICK KITCHEN TOWELS . . .

AND CAREFULLY TILT IT TO TURN OUT THE LOAF.

IF IT DOESN'T COME OUT EASILY, A HARD RAP ON THE COUNTER CAN HELP.

OR USE A FOLDED KITCHEN TOWEL TO FIRMLY GRAB ONE EDGE OF THE PAN WITH ONE HAND, AND USE YOUR OTHER HAND TO PRY THE LOAF OUT.

(AND MAYBE USE MORE COOKING SPRAY NEXT TIME.)

LET THE LOAF COOL ON A RACK FOR AT LEAST 30 MINUTES BEFORE SLICING; 1 HOUR IS BETTER.

A RIFF ON THE STANDARD:
THE STANDARD #2

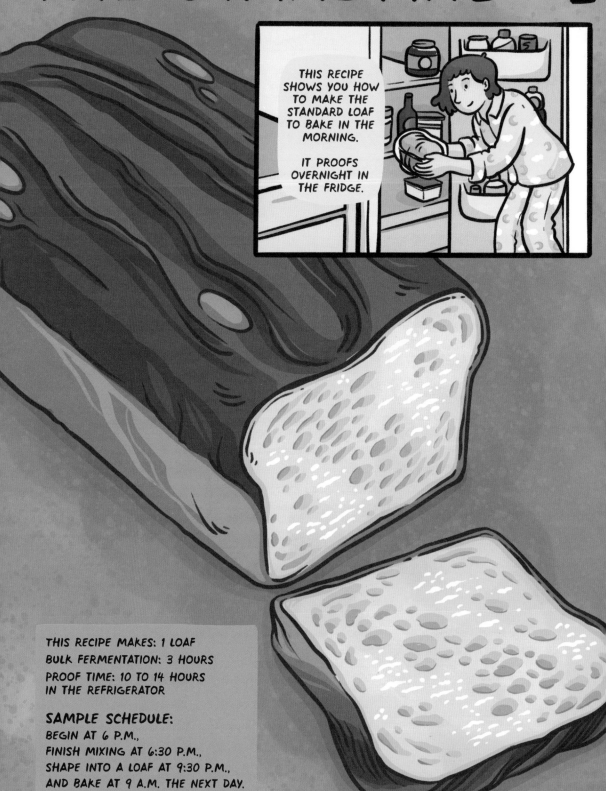

THIS RECIPE SHOWS YOU HOW TO MAKE THE STANDARD LOAF TO BAKE IN THE MORNING.

IT PROOFS OVERNIGHT IN THE FRIDGE.

THIS RECIPE MAKES: 1 LOAF
BULK FERMENTATION: 3 HOURS
PROOF TIME: 10 TO 14 HOURS IN THE REFRIGERATOR

SAMPLE SCHEDULE:
BEGIN AT 6 P.M.,
FINISH MIXING AT 6:30 P.M.,
SHAPE INTO A LOAF AT 9:30 P.M.,
AND BAKE AT 9 A.M. THE NEXT DAY.

INGREDIENT	QUANTITY		BAKER'S %
WHITE FLOUR	400G	2 ¾ CUPS + 2 TSP	80%
WHOLE-WHEAT FLOUR	100G	⅔ CUP + 1 TBSP + 1 ¼ TSP	20%
WATER	380G 90° TO 95°F / 32° TO 35°C	1 ½ CUPS + 1 TBSP + 1 TSP	76%
FINE SEA SALT	11G	2 ¼ TSP	2.2%
INSTANT DRIED YEAST	3G	3/4 TSP	0.6%
LEVAIN (OPTIONAL)	100G	1/2 CUP	9% OF TOTAL FLOUR

1: AUTOLYSE

MEASURE 380 GRAMS (90° TO 95°F / 32° TO 35°C) WATER INTO A 6-QUART ROUND TUB OR SIMILAR CONTAINER.

IF YOU HAVE A LEVAIN, ADD 100 GRAMS FROM THE REFRIGERATOR.

YOU CAN WEIGH IT DIRECTLY INTO THE DOUGH TUB WITH ITS WATER.

STIR A BIT WITH YOUR FINGERS TO LOOSEN UP THE CULTURE.

ADD 400 GRAMS WHITE BREAD FLOUR AND 100 GRAMS WHOLE-WHEAT FLOUR.

MIX IT BY HAND UNTIL ALL IS INCORPORATED.

SPRINKLE 11 GRAMS FINE SEA SALT AND 3 GRAMS INSTANT DRIED YEAST EVENLY ACROSS THE TOP OF THE AUTOLYSE DOUGH.

LET THEM REST THERE, WHERE THEY WILL PARTIALLY DISSOLVE.

COVER AND LET REST FOR 15 TO 20 MINUTES.

THE STEPS FOR MIX AND FOLD AND FIRST RISE ARE THE SAME AS FOR THE STANDARD LOAF, PAGES 88–90.

INSTEAD OF ABOUT 3½ HOURS FOR THE FIRST RISE, THIS DOUGH'S RISE TAKES ABOUT 3 HOURS.

2: MIX

3: FOLD & FIRST RISE

IF YOU HAVE A MARKED 6-QUART DOUGH TUB, THE DOUGH IS READY TO REMOVE WHEN IT HAS RISEN TO ½ INCH BELOW THE 2-QUART LINE.

IF THE ROOM IS COOL AND THE DOUGH IS TAKING LONGER, LET IT CONTINUE TO RISE UNTIL IT REACHES THIS AMOUNT OF RISE.

STEPS 4 AND 5 ARE THE SAME AS THE STANDARD.

4: REMOVE THE DOUGH FROM ITS TUB

5: SHAPE

6: PROOF

USE YOUR HAND TO APPLY A LIGHT FILM OF WATER ACROSS THE ENTIRE TOP SURFACE OF THE DOUGH.

PUNCH IT DOWN!

WET YOUR HAND, MAKE A FIST, AND PUNCH DOWN THE DOUGH WHILE IT'S IN THE BAKING PAN TO REDUCE ITS VOLUME A BIT.

PLACE YOUR BREAD PAN IN A PLASTIC BAG, THEN REFRIGERATE IT.

LEAVE A FEW INCHES OF ROOM AT THE TOP FOR THE DOUGH TO EXPAND, AND TUCK THE BAG UNDER THE PAN.

THE POINT OF THE BAG IS TO KEEP THE DOUGH FROM DRYING OUT DURING THE PROOF TIME. KEEP IT AIRTIGHT.

THE IDEAL TIMING FOR THIS COLD PROOF IS 10 TO 14 HOURS IN THE REFRIGERATOR.

WITH MY USUAL BREAD PAN (8½" BY 4½" BY 2¾"), I LIKE TO SEE THE DOUGH RISING A BIT ABOVE THE RIM OF THE PAN BEFORE BAKING.

IF YOUR PAN IS LARGER, THE DOUGH LIKELY WON'T RISE ABOVE ITS RIM.

7: PREHEAT

ABOUT 45 MINUTES PRIOR TO BAKING, POSITION A RACK IN THE MIDDLE OF THE OVEN AND PREHEAT THE OVEN TO 450°F / 230°C.

8: BAKE

LEAVE THE LOAF IN THE REFRIGERATOR UNTIL THE OVEN IS PREHEATED AND IT'S TIME TO BAKE!

REMOVE THE LOAF FROM THE FRIDGE, AND PEEL OFF THE PLASTIC BAG.

SOMETIMES A LITTLE BIT OF DOUGH STICKS TO THE BAG . . .

BUT IF YOU'VE PUT THAT FILM OF WATER ON THE TOP OF THE DOUGH JUST BEFORE COVERING IT, THE BAG SHOULD PEEL RIGHT OFF.

PLACE THE PAN ON THE CENTER OF THE MIDDLE RACK IN THE OVEN.

TURN DOWN THE HEAT TO 425°F / 220°C. SET A TIMER FOR 50 MINUTES, AND CHECK THE BREAD AT ABOUT 40 TO 45 MINUTES.

BAKE UNTIL THE TOP HAS A DARK BROWN COLOR ALL AROUND IT.

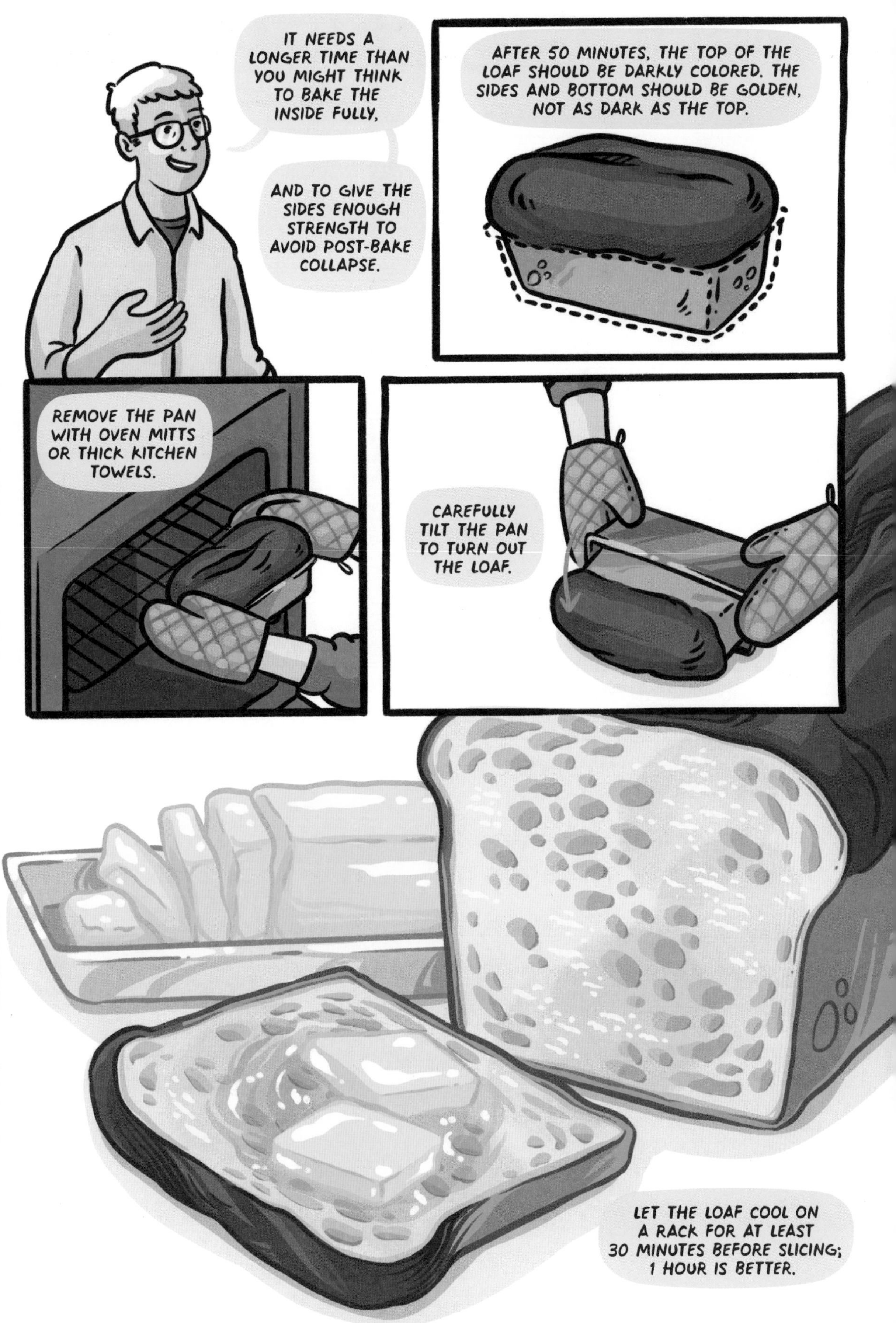
IT NEEDS A LONGER TIME THAN YOU MIGHT THINK TO BAKE THE INSIDE FULLY,
AND TO GIVE THE SIDES ENOUGH STRENGTH TO AVOID POST-BAKE COLLAPSE.
AFTER 50 MINUTES, THE TOP OF THE LOAF SHOULD BE DARKLY COLORED. THE SIDES AND BOTTOM SHOULD BE GOLDEN, NOT AS DARK AS THE TOP.
REMOVE THE PAN WITH OVEN MITTS OR THICK KITCHEN TOWELS.
CAREFULLY TILT THE PAN TO TURN OUT THE LOAF.
LET THE LOAF COOL ON A RACK FOR AT LEAST 30 MINUTES BEFORE SLICING; 1 HOUR IS BETTER.

MULTIGRAIN BREAD

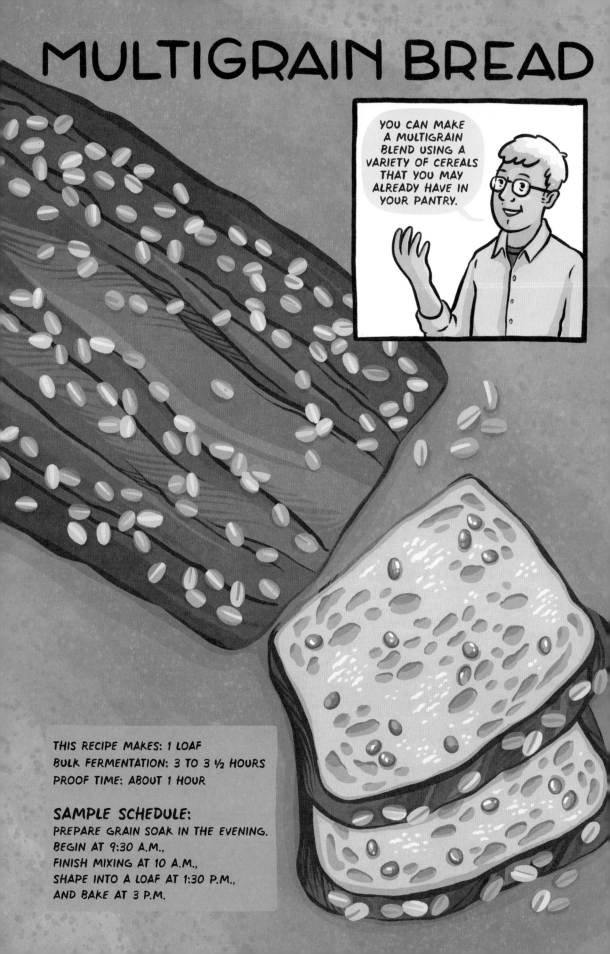

THIS RECIPE MAKES: 1 LOAF
BULK FERMENTATION: 3 TO 3 ½ HOURS
PROOF TIME: ABOUT 1 HOUR

SAMPLE SCHEDULE:
PREPARE GRAIN SOAK IN THE EVENING.
BEGIN AT 9:30 A.M.,
FINISH MIXING AT 10 A.M.,
SHAPE INTO A LOAF AT 1:30 P.M.,
AND BAKE AT 3 P.M.

IN THIS RECIPE, WE USE ROLLED OATS, ROLLED BARLEY, AND BUCKWHEAT GROATS.

USING ONLY ONE GRAIN, LIKE ROLLED HEIRLOOM BARLEY, CAN WORK TOO.

WHILE I MAKE THIS AS A PAN BREAD, IT WORKS GREAT AS A DUTCH OVEN BREAD TOO.

THE DRIED GRAINS NEED TO BE SOAKED FOR 6 HOURS UP TO OVERNIGHT BEFORE THEY GO INTO THE DOUGH.

A SHORTER SOAK GIVES BUCKWHEAT GROATS A LITTLE BIT OF "TOOTH," WHICH I'VE DISCOVERED THAT I LIKE.

ONE KEY TO THIS RECIPE IS USING THE SOAKING LIQUID IN THE DOUGH.

IT HAS A MILKY COLOR AND TASTES MILDLY OF THE GRAINS.

I ALSO LIKE TO TOP THE BREAD WITH ROLLED OATS BECAUSE THEY LOOK NICE.

INGREDIENT	QUANTITY		BAKER'S %
WHITE FLOUR	280G	2 CUPS	70%
WHOLE-WHEAT OR WHOLE-SPELT FLOUR	120G	¾ CUP + 2 TBSP + 2 ¼ TSP	30%
WATER	70G 90° TO 95°F / 32° TO 35°C	¼ CUP + 2 TBSP	17.5%
BUCKWHEAT/BARLEY/OAT SOAKING LIQUID	225G 70°F (21°C)	¾ CUP + 3 TBSP	56.25%
FINE SEA SALT	14G	2 ¾ TSP	3.5%
INSTANT DRIED YEAST	3G	¾ TSP	0.75%
HONEY	15G	2 TSP	3.75%
BUCKWHEAT GROATS	40G	3 TBSP + 1 ¾ TSP	10%
ROLLED BARLEY	40G	¼ CUP + 2 TBSP + 1 ¼ TSP	10%
ROLLED OATS (FOR THE DOUGH)	40G	¼ CUP + 2 TBSP + 1 ¼ TSP	10%
ROLLED OATS (FOR TOPPING THE LOAF)	15G	2 TBSP + 1 ¼ TSP	
LEVAIN (OPTIONAL)	100G	½ CUP	9% OF TOTAL FLOUR

1A: SOAK THE GRAINS

MEASURE 40 GRAMS EACH OF THE BUCKWHEAT GROATS, ROLLED BARLEY, AND ROLLED OATS (OR 120 GRAMS OF JUST ONE GRAIN) INTO A CONTAINER.

COVER WITH COLD WATER.

LET IT SIT OUT AT ROOM TEMPERATURE OVERNIGHT (OR ONLY 6 TO 8 HOURS IF YOU WANT A LITTLE MORE TEXTURE).

THE NEXT MORNING, STRAIN THE SOAKED GRAINS THROUGH A FINE-MESH STRAINER SET OVER A BOWL...

AND FIRMLY PRESS AGAINST THE GRAINS TO REMOVE AS MUCH LIQUID AS POSSIBLE.

RESERVE THE SOAKING LIQUID FOR THE DOUGH.

1B: AUTOLYSE

MEASURE 225 GRAMS OF THE SOAKING LIQUID INTO A 6-QUART ROUND TUB OR SIMILAR CONTAINER.

ADD 70 GRAMS (90° TO 95°F / 32° TO 35°C) WATER.

IF YOU HAVE A LEVAIN, ADD 100 GRAMS FROM THE REFRIGERATOR, AND STIR A BIT WITH YOUR FINGERS TO LOOSEN UP THE CULTURE.

ADD 280 GRAMS WHITE BREAD FLOUR AND 120 GRAMS WHOLE-WHEAT OR WHOLE-SPELT FLOUR.

ADD ALL THE SOAKED GRAINS.

MIX IT BY HAND UNTIL ALL IS INCORPORATED.

IT'S GOING TO BE A PRETTY WET DOUGH, SO DON'T WORRY ABOUT THAT.

PUT 2 TEASPOONS (15 GRAMS) HONEY ON ONE SIDE OF THE TOP OF THE DOUGH . . .

AND SPRINKLE 14 GRAMS FINE SEA SALT EVENLY ACROSS THE OTHER SIDE.

THEN SPRINKLE 3 GRAMS INSTANT DRIED YEAST ON TOP OF THE SALT.

LET THEM REST THERE, WHERE THEY WILL PARTIALLY DISSOLVE.

COVER AND LET REST FOR 15 TO 20 MINUTES.

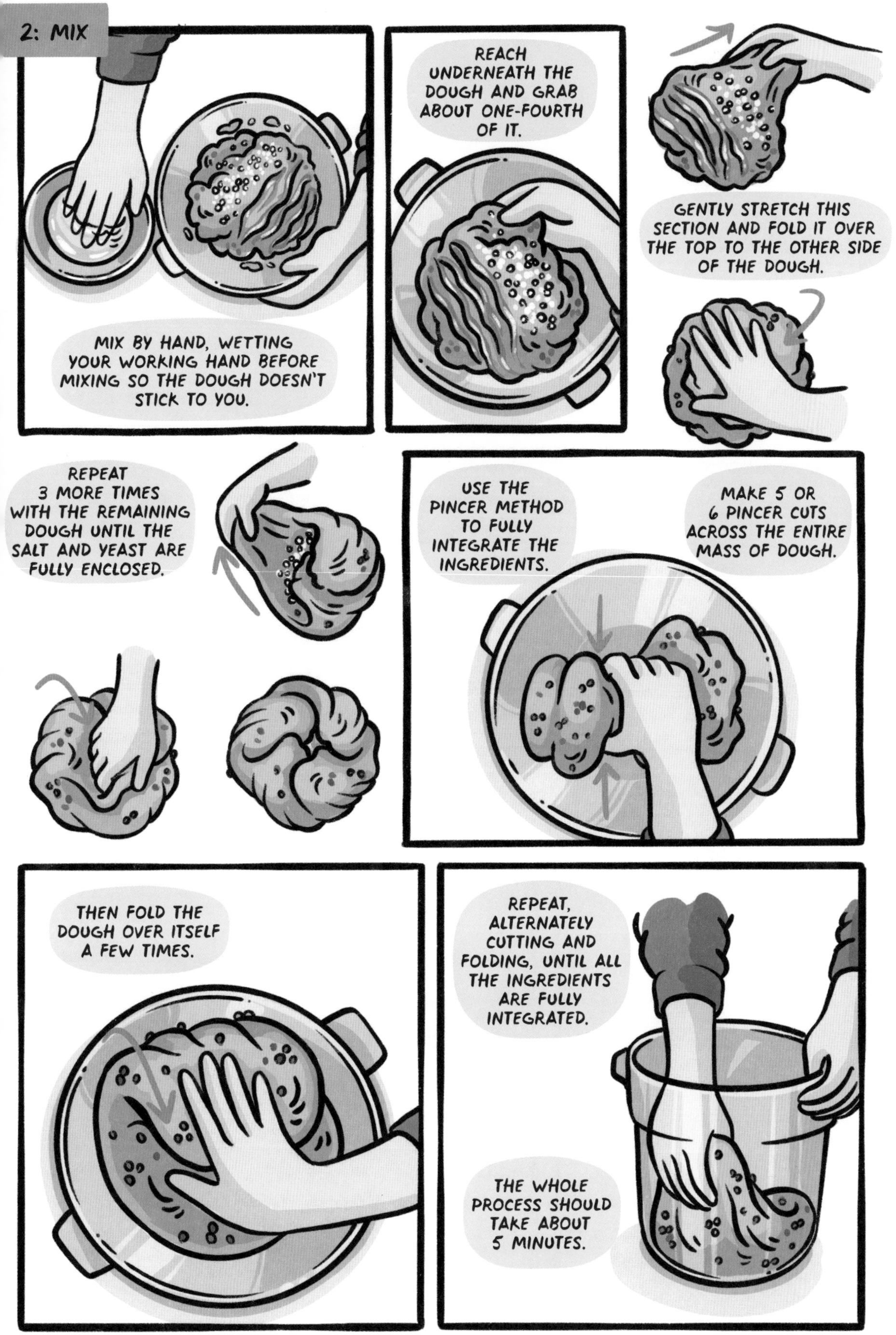

2: MIX
MIX BY HAND, WETTING YOUR WORKING HAND BEFORE MIXING SO THE DOUGH DOESN'T STICK TO YOU.
REACH UNDERNEATH THE DOUGH AND GRAB ABOUT ONE-FOURTH OF IT.
GENTLY STRETCH THIS SECTION AND FOLD IT OVER THE TOP TO THE OTHER SIDE OF THE DOUGH.
REPEAT 3 MORE TIMES WITH THE REMAINING DOUGH UNTIL THE SALT AND YEAST ARE FULLY ENCLOSED.
USE THE PINCER METHOD TO FULLY INTEGRATE THE INGREDIENTS.
MAKE 5 OR 6 PINCER CUTS ACROSS THE ENTIRE MASS OF DOUGH.
THEN FOLD THE DOUGH OVER ITSELF A FEW TIMES.
REPEAT, ALTERNATELY CUTTING AND FOLDING, UNTIL ALL THE INGREDIENTS ARE FULLY INTEGRATED.
THE WHOLE PROCESS SHOULD TAKE ABOUT 5 MINUTES.

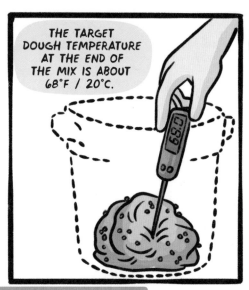

THE TARGET DOUGH TEMPERATURE AT THE END OF THE MIX IS ABOUT 68°F / 20°C.

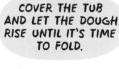

THIS DOUGH MIXES COOLER BECAUSE OF THE ROOM-TEMPERATURE SOAKING LIQUID.

COVER THE TUB AND LET THE DOUGH RISE UNTIL IT'S TIME TO FOLD.

3: FOLD & FIRST RISE

THIS DOUGH NEEDS 2 FOLDS. IT'S EASIEST TO APPLY THE FOLDS DURING THE FIRST HOUR AFTER MIXING THE DOUGH.

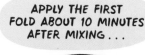

APPLY THE FIRST FOLD ABOUT 10 MINUTES AFTER MIXING . . .

AND THE SECOND AFTER YOU SEE THE DOUGH SPREAD OUT IN THE TUB.

IT'S OK TO FOLD LATER; JUST BE SURE TO LEAVE THE DOUGH ALONE FOR THE LAST HOUR OF RISING.

WHEN THE DOUGH IS 2½ TO 3 TIMES ITS ORIGINAL VOLUME, ABOUT 3 HOURS AFTER THE MIX, IT'S READY TO BE MADE UP INTO A LOAF.

IF YOU ARE USING A 6-QUART DOUGH TUB, THE IDEAL POINT IS WHEN THE EDGE OF THE DOUGH HAS REACHED JUST SHY OF THE 2-QUART LINE ON THE SIDE OF THE TUB.

AND THE DOUGH WILL BE SLIGHTLY DOMED – NOT FLATTENED, NOT COLLAPSED.

IF IT REACHES THE 2-QUART LINE ON YOUR DOUGH TUB, THAT'S FINE TOO, BUT DON'T LET IT GO BEYOND THAT.

IF THE ROOM IS COOL AND THE DOUGH IS TAKING LONGER, LET THE DOUGH CONTINUE TO RISE UNTIL IT REACHES THIS AMOUNT OF VOLUME EXPANSION.

IF YOU'RE NOT USING A MARKED DOUGH TUB, YOU'LL HAVE TO EYEBALL IT. USE YOUR BEST JUDGMENT.

4: REMOVE THE DOUGH FROM ITS TUB

LIGHTLY FLOUR A WORK SURFACE ABOUT 12 INCHES WIDE.

FLOUR YOUR HANDS . . .

AND SPRINKLE A BIT OF FLOUR AROUND THE EDGES OF THE TUB.

TIP THE TUB SLIGHTLY AND GENTLY WORK YOUR FLOURED FREE HAND BENEATH THE DOUGH TO LOOSEN IT FROM THE BOTTOM OF THE TUB.

THEN TURN THE TUB ON ITS SIDE AND EASE THE DOUGH OUT ONTO THE WORK SURFACE WITHOUT PULLING OR TEARING IT.

EVEN IF YOUR BREAD PAN IS NONSTICK, I HIGHLY RECOMMEND GIVING IT A LIGHT SPRITZ OF COOKING SPRAY.

5: SHAPE

WITH FLOURED HANDS, PICK UP THE DOUGH AND EASE IT BACK ONTO THE WORK SURFACE IN A SOMEWHAT EVEN, RECTANGULAR SHAPE.

STRETCH THE DOUGH, SIMULTANEOUSLY PULLING IT RIGHT AND LEFT UNTIL IT RESISTS . . .

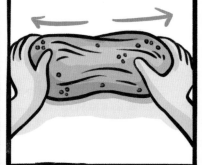

AND THEN FOLD THE ENDS BACK OVER EACH OTHER, CREATING A "PACKET" THE WIDTH OF YOUR BAKING PAN.

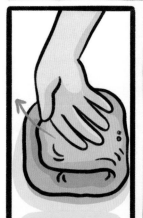

BRUSH OFF ANY LOOSE FLOUR FROM THE TOP OF THE DOUGH . . .

AND DO A ROLL-UP MOTION FROM THE BOTTOM UP OR FROM TOP TO BOTTOM TO FORM A TUBE OF DOUGH THAT'S ABOUT THE SAME WIDTH AS YOUR BAKING PAN.

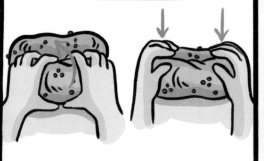

PLACE THE DOUGH SEAM SIDE UP INTO THE PAN.

FOR THE ROLLED-OATS TOPPING, APPLY A THIN FILM OF WATER WITH YOUR HAND TO COVER THE ENTIRE TOP OF THE LOAF.

SPRINKLE 15 GRAMS OATS TO COVER THE LOAF . . .

AND PAT THEM DOWN FIRMLY.

6: PROOF

PLACE YOUR BREAD PAN IN A PLASTIC BAG.

LEAVE A FEW INCHES FOR THE DOUGH TO EXPAND, AND TUCK THE BAG UNDER THE PAN.

ASSUMING YOUR ROOM TEMPERATURE IS ABOUT 70°F / 21°C, PLAN ON BAKING THE LOAF ABOUT 1½ HOURS AFTER IT IS SHAPED.

THIS LOAF ONLY NEEDS TO RISE TO THE TOP OF THE PAN BEFORE BAKING; IT WILL GET A GENEROUS SPRING IN THE OVEN.

ABOUT 45 MINUTES PRIOR TO BAKING, POSITION A RACK IN THE MIDDLE OF THE OVEN . . .

AND PREHEAT THE OVEN TO 450°F / 230°C.

8: BAKE

REMOVE THE PAN FROM THE PLASTIC BAG AND PLACE IT ON THE CENTER OF THE MIDDLE RACK.

TURN DOWN THE HEAT TO 425°F / 220°C AND BAKE.

AFTER 30 MINUTES, CHECK FOR EVEN BAKING (GIVE THE PAN A TURN IF THE BAKING IS UNEVEN) AND BAKE FOR ANOTHER 25 TO 30 MINUTES.

THIS DOUGH HAS MORE WATER THAN TRADITIONAL PAN LOAVES . . .

SO IT NEEDS A LONGER TIME THAN YOU MIGHT THINK TO BAKE THE INSIDE AND TO COLOR THE SIDES AND GIVE THEM STRENGTH.

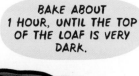

BAKE ABOUT 1 HOUR, UNTIL THE TOP OF THE LOAF IS VERY DARK.

PAY CLOSE ATTENTION TO THE FINAL 10 MINUTES OF THE BAKE.

THE SIDES AND BOTTOM SHOULD NOT BE AS DARK AS THE TOP.

REMOVE THE PAN WITH OVEN MITTS OR THICK KITCHEN TOWELS . . .

AND CAREFULLY TILT IT TO TURN OUT THE LOAF.

LET THE LOAF COOL ON A RACK FOR AT LEAST 30 MINUTES BEFORE SLICING; 1 HOUR IS BETTER.

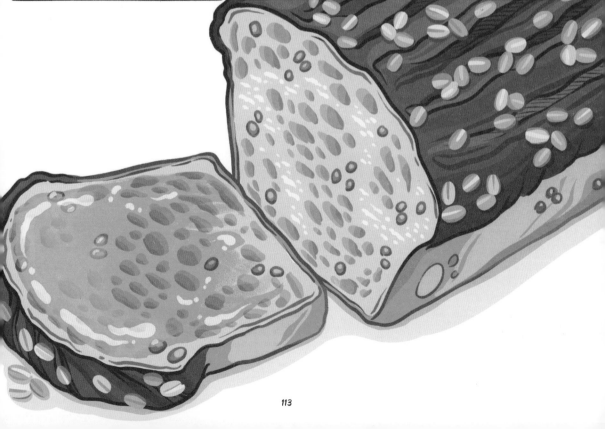

COUNTRY BREAD

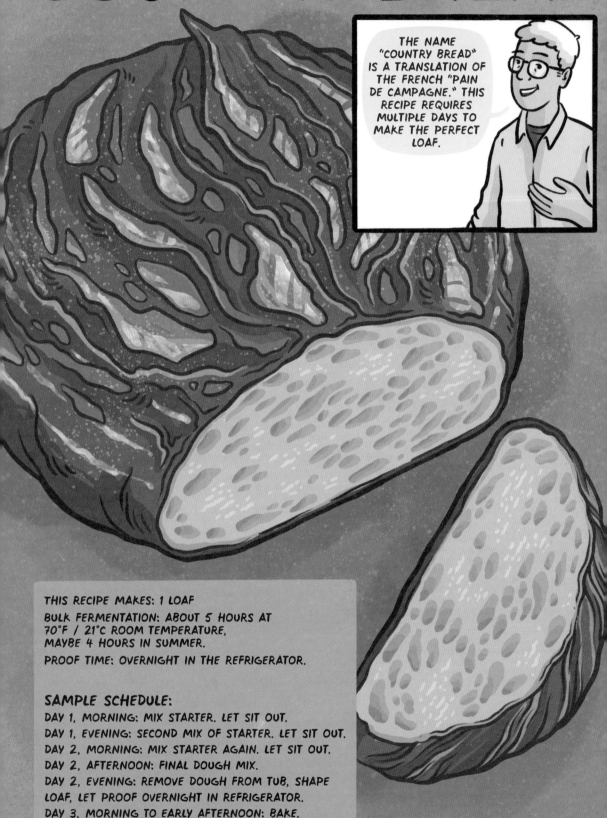

THE NAME "COUNTRY BREAD" IS A TRANSLATION OF THE FRENCH "PAIN DE CAMPAGNE." THIS RECIPE REQUIRES MULTIPLE DAYS TO MAKE THE PERFECT LOAF.

THIS RECIPE MAKES: 1 LOAF

BULK FERMENTATION: ABOUT 5 HOURS AT 70°F / 21°C ROOM TEMPERATURE, MAYBE 4 HOURS IN SUMMER.

PROOF TIME: OVERNIGHT IN THE REFRIGERATOR.

SAMPLE SCHEDULE:

DAY 1, MORNING: MIX STARTER. LET SIT OUT.

DAY 1, EVENING: SECOND MIX OF STARTER. LET SIT OUT.

DAY 2, MORNING: MIX STARTER AGAIN. LET SIT OUT.

DAY 2, AFTERNOON: FINAL DOUGH MIX.

DAY 2, EVENING: REMOVE DOUGH FROM TUB, SHAPE LOAF, LET PROOF OVERNIGHT IN REFRIGERATOR.

DAY 3, MORNING TO EARLY AFTERNOON: BAKE.

THIS LOAF HAS A RUSTIC LOOK AND A ROUGHER BLEND OF FLOURS THAN A PURE-WHITE CITY BREAD.

THE FLOUR BLEND OF A COUNTRY BREAD IS UP TO THE BAKER . . .

AND THE LEAVENING WILL BE ENTIRELY OR MOSTLY FROM A LEVAIN.

IT SHOULD BE DELICIOUS, CRUSTY, AND THE OPPOSITE OF A FINE WHITE BREAD.

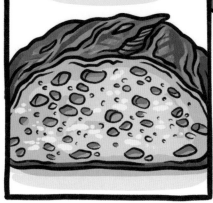

THE STARTER BUILDS ARE QUICK, SIMPLE MIXES THAT CAN BE DONE IN JUST A COUPLE MINUTES.

I USE THREE FEEDS TO BUILD UP THE STARTER.

THIS ALLOWS THE CULTURE TO GIVE A GOOD RISE TO THE BREAD AND A GOOD BALANCE OF FLAVORS WITHOUT BEING TOO SOUR.

BAKING WITH A NATURALLY LEAVENED CULTURE IS MORE WORK THAN WITH STRAIGHT YEASTED DOUGHS, BUT THE RESULT IS WORTH IT!

STARTER: DAY 1, MORNING

INGREDIENT	QUANTITY		
LEVAIN	50 TO 60G	1/4 CUP	
WHITE FLOUR	100G	½ CUP + 3 TBSP + 1¼ TSP	
WATER	100G 75° TO 80°F / 24° TO 27°C IN SUMMER; 85°F / 29°C IN WINTER	¼ CUP + 2 TBSP + 2 TSP	

STARTER: DAY 1, EVENING

INGREDIENT	QUANTITY		
MORNING STARTER MIX	ALL OF IT		
WHITE FLOUR	100G	½ CUP + 3 TBSP + 1¼ TSP	
WATER	100G 70°F / 21°C IN SUMMER; 85°F / 29°C IN WINTER	¼ CUP + 2 TBSP + 2 TSP	

STARTER: DAY 2, MORNING

INGREDIENT	QUANTITY		
STARTER	50 TO 60G IN SUMMER; 75G IN WINTER	¼ CUP IN SUMMER; ¼ CUP + 2 TBSP IN WINTER	
WHITE FLOUR	100G	½ CUP + 3 TBSP + 1¼ TSP	
WATER	100G 90° TO 95°F / 32° TO 35°C	¼ CUP + 2 TBSP + 2 TSP	

FINAL DOUGH: DAY 2, AFTERNOON

INGREDIENT	QUANTITY		BAKER'S %
WHITE FLOUR	295G	2 CUPS + 1 TBSP + 2¼ TSP	79%
WHOLE-WHEAT FLOUR	80G	½ CUP + 1 TBSP + ½ TSP	16%
WHOLE OR DARK RYE FLOUR	25G	3 TBSP + ¼ TSP	5%
WATER	300G 90° TO 95°F / 32° TO 35°C	1¼ CUPS	80%
FINE SEA SALT	11G	2¼ TSP	2.2%
STARTER	200G	1¼ CUPS	20%

TO BEGIN THE STARTER, WEIGH AN EMPTY 2-QUART CONTAINER OR A BIG BOWL.

MARK ITS WEIGHT ON THE CONTAINER'S SIDE OR WRITE IT DOWN. YOU WILL NEED THIS INFO LATER.

MEASURE 100 GRAMS (75° TO 80°F / 24° TO 27°C IN SUMMER; 85°F / 29°C IN WINTER) WATER INTO YOUR CONTAINER.

ADD 50 TO 60 GRAMS LEVAIN FROM THE REFRIGERATOR AND STIR A BIT WITH YOUR FINGERS TO LOOSEN UP THE CULTURE.

ADD 100 GRAMS WHITE BREAD FLOUR AND MIX WITH YOUR FINGERS UNTIL ALL IS INCORPORATED.

COVER WITH A LID OR PLASTIC WRAP, AND LEAVE IT OUT AT ROOM TEMPERATURE.

THIS WORKS WELL AT 70°F / 21°C ROOM TEMPERATURE.

IF YOUR KITCHEN IS MUCH WARMER THAN THAT, SAY, 75° TO 80°F / 24° TO 27°C, USE COOLER WATER AT 65° TO 70°F / 18° TO 21°C.

PUT THE REST OF YOUR LEVAIN BACK INTO THE FRIDGE.

KEEP ALL THE MORNING STARTER MIX.

MEASURE 100 GRAMS (70°F / 21°C IN SUMMER; 85°F / 29°C IN WINTER) WATER AND 100 GRAMS WHITE BREAD FLOUR INTO THE SAME CONTAINER ON TOP OF THE STARTER MIX.

MIX WITH YOUR FINGERS UNTIL ALL IS INCORPORATED.

COVER WITH THE LID OR PLASTIC WRAP.

LEAVE IT OUT AT ROOM TEMPERATURE (65° TO 70°F / 18° TO 21°C) UNTIL THE NEXT MORNING.

IF IT IS SUMMER, AND YOUR KITCHEN IS MUCH WARMER THAN THAT THROUGH THE NIGHT, E.G., 75° TO 80°F / 24° TO 27°C . . .

IT NEEDS TO BE COOLER THAN THE PREVIOUS FEEDING . . .

USE COOLER WATER AGAIN, THIS TIME ABOUT 60°F / 16°C.

BECAUSE THE REST OF THE STARTER IS ALREADY AT A WARM ROOM TEMPERATURE.

AROUND 8 A.M., REFERENCE THE EMPTY CONTAINER WEIGHT AND REMOVE ALL BUT 50 TO 60 GRAMS (75 GRAMS IN WINTER) OF THE DAY 1 STARTER FROM YOUR CONTAINER.

YOU CAN TOSS THE REST, OR USE IT TO MAKE THE EXCELLENT PIZZA DOUGHS ON PAGES 143 AND 146.

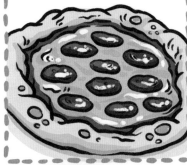

MEASURE 100 GRAMS (95°F / 35°C) WATER INTO THE CONTAINER WITH THE STARTER AND MIX WITH YOUR FINGERS UNTIL YOU HAVE A SLURRY.

ADD 100 GRAMS WHITE BREAD FLOUR. MIX WITH YOUR FINGERS UNTIL ALL IS INCORPORATED.

KEEP IN A WARM PLACE, 70° TO 75°F / 21° TO 24° C.

A VISUAL CUE THAT THE STARTER IS READY FOR THIS NEXT PHASE IS THAT AT A CERTAIN POINT, THERE WILL BE SOME SMALL BUBBLES AT THE TOP.

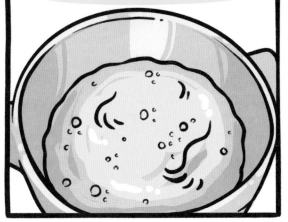

ABOUT AN HOUR LATER, THE WHOLE TOP WILL BE COVERED IN LITTLE BUBBLES. IT IS AT THIS SECOND BUBBLY STAGE THAT THE STARTER IS READY.

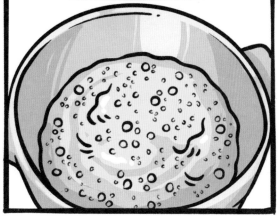

YOU WILL FEEL ITS LIGHT AND GASSY TEXTURE WHEN YOU REMOVE IT TO PUT IT INTO YOUR FINAL DOUGH MIX.

IT WILL REMAIN USABLE FOR A COUPLE HOURS BEFORE STARTING TO DEVELOP MORE SOUR FLAVORS.

1: AUTOLYSE

MEASURE 300 GRAMS (90° TO 95°F / 32° TO 35°C) WATER INTO A 6-QUART ROUND TUB OR SIMILAR CONTAINER.

WET YOUR HAND AND ADD 200 GRAMS OF THE DAY 2 STARTER YOU MIXED IN THE MORNING.

STIR A BIT WITH YOUR FINGERS TO LOOSEN UP THE CULTURE.

ADD 295 GRAMS WHITE BREAD FLOUR, 80 GRAMS WHOLE-WHEAT FLOUR, AND 25 GRAMS RYE FLOUR.

MIX IT BY HAND UNTIL ALL IS INCORPORATED.

SPRINKLE 11 GRAMS FINE SEA SALT EVENLY ACROSS THE TOP OF THE AUTOLYSE DOUGH. LET IT REST THERE, WHERE IT WILL PARTIALLY DISSOLVE.

COVER AND LET REST FOR 20 MINUTES.

WET YOUR WORKING HAND BEFORE MIXING SO THE DOUGH DOESN'T STICK TO YOU.

REACH UNDERNEATH THE DOUGH AND GRAB ABOUT ONE-FOURTH OF IT.

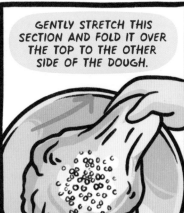

GENTLY STRETCH THIS SECTION AND FOLD IT OVER THE TOP TO THE OTHER SIDE OF THE DOUGH.

REPEAT 3 MORE TIMES WITH THE REMAINING DOUGH UNTIL THE SALT IS FULLY ENCLOSED.

MAKE 5 OR 6 PINCER CUTS ACROSS THE ENTIRE MASS OF DOUGH.

THEN FOLD THE DOUGH OVER ITSELF A FEW TIMES.

REPEAT, ALTERNATELY CUTTING AND FOLDING, UNTIL ALL THE INGREDIENTS ARE FULLY INTEGRATED.

COVER AND LET THE DOUGH REST FOR A FEW MINUTES . . .

THEN FOLD FOR ANOTHER 30 SECONDS, OR UNTIL THE DOUGH TIGHTENS UP.

THE WHOLE PROCESS SHOULD TAKE ABOUT 5 MINUTES.

THE TARGET DOUGH TEMPERATURE AT THE END OF THE MIX IS 75°F / 24°C.

COVER THE TUB AND LET THE DOUGH RISE UNTIL THE NEXT FOLD.

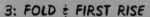

3: FOLD & FIRST RISE

THIS DOUGH NEEDS 3 FOLDS.

IT'S EASIEST TO APPLY THE FOLDS DURING THE FIRST 1½ HOURS AFTER MIXING THE DOUGH.

APPLY THE FIRST FOLD ABOUT 10 MINUTES AFTER MIXING . . .

AND THE SECOND AND THIRD WHEN YOU SEE THE DOUGH SPREAD OUT IN THE TUB FROM THE PREVIOUS FOLD.

IF NEED BE, IT'S OK TO FOLD LATER; JUST BE SURE TO LEAVE IT ALONE FOR THE LAST HOUR OF RISING.

WHEN THE DOUGH IS ABOUT 2½ TIMES ITS ORIGINAL VOLUME, AND THE EDGE OF THE DOUGH IS ABOUT ½ INCH BELOW THE 2-QUART LINE IN THE DOUGH TUB, IT'S READY TO BE MADE UP INTO A LOAF.

IF IT IS IN A ROOM AT 70°F / 21°C, THIS FIRST FERMENT SHOULD TAKE 4 TO 5 HOURS.

IF YOUR KITCHEN IS WARMER OR COLDER THAN MINE, YOUR TIME WILL VARY, SO KEEP AN EYE ON THE VOLUME EXPANSION TO MAKE THE CALL.

JUDGE WHEN IT'S READY BASED ON VOLUME EXPANSION MORE THAN TIME.

IF YOU'RE NOT USING A MARKED DOUGH TUB, YOU'LL HAVE TO EYEBALL IT. USE YOUR BEST JUDGMENT.

DAY 2, EVENING **4: REMOVE THE DOUGH FROM ITS TUB**

LIGHTLY FLOUR A WORK SURFACE ABOUT 12 INCHES WIDE.

FLOUR YOUR HANDS.

SPRINKLE A BIT OF FLOUR AROUND THE EDGES OF THE TUB.

TIP THE TUB SLIGHTLY, AND GENTLY WORK YOUR FLOURED FREE HAND BENEATH THE DOUGH TO LOOSEN IT FROM THE BOTTOM OF THE TUB.

THEN TURN THE TUB ON ITS SIDE AND EASE THE DOUGH OUT ONTO THE WORK SURFACE WITHOUT PULLING OR TEARING IT.

5: SHAPE

DUST A PROOFING BASKET MODERATELY WITH FLOUR AND SPREAD THE FLOUR AROUND WITH YOUR HAND.

SHAPE THE DOUGH INTO A MEDIUM-TIGHT BALL FOLLOWING THE INSTRUCTIONS ON PAGE 34.

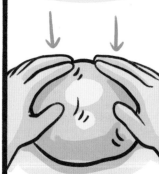

PLACE IT SEAM SIDE DOWN IN ITS PROOFING BASKET.

6: PROOF

PLACE THE BASKET IN A PLASTIC BAG, AND TUCK THE BAG UNDER THE BASKET.

REFRIGERATE OVERNIGHT.

THE NEXT MORNING, 12 TO 16 HOURS AFTER THE LOAF WENT INTO THE REFRIGERATOR, IT SHOULD BE READY TO BAKE.

IT DOES NOT NEED TO COME TO ROOM TEMPERATURE FIRST.

DAY 3, MORNING TO EARLY AFTERNOON

ABOUT 45 MINUTES PRIOR TO BAKING, POSITION A RACK IN THE MIDDLE OF THE OVEN . . .

7: PREHEAT

AND PUT A DUTCH OVEN, WITH ITS LID, ON THE RACK.

PREHEAT THE OVEN TO 475°F / 245°C.

8: BAKE

INVERT THE BASKET WITH ITS PROOFED LOAF ONTO A LIGHTLY FLOURED COUNTERTOP.

GIVE THE BASKET A FIRM TAP ON THE COUNTERTOP TO POP THE DOUGH OUT.

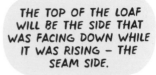

THE TOP OF THE LOAF WILL BE THE SIDE THAT WAS FACING DOWN WHILE IT WAS RISING — THE SEAM SIDE.

FOR THE NEXT STEP, PLEASE BE CAREFUL NOT TO LET YOUR HANDS, FINGERS, OR FOREARMS TOUCH THE EXTREMELY HOT DUTCH OVEN.

USE OVEN MITTS TO REMOVE THE PREHEATED DUTCH OVEN FROM YOUR OVEN.

REMOVE THE LID . . .

AND CAREFULLY PLACE THE LOAF SEAM SIDE UP IN THE HOT DUTCH OVEN.

USE THE MITTS TO REPLACE THE LID . . .

RETURN THE DUTCH OVEN TO THE CENTER OF THE MIDDLE RACK, AND BAKE FOR 30 MINUTES.

THEN CAREFULLY REMOVE THE LID . . .

AND BAKE FOR ABOUT 20 MINUTES MORE, UNTIL DARK BROWN ALL AROUND THE LOAF.

CHECK AFTER 15 MINUTES OF BAKING UNCOVERED IN CASE YOUR OVEN RUNS HOT.

REMOVE THE DUTCH OVEN AND CAREFULLY TILT IT TO TURN THE LOAF OUT.

LET THE LOAF COOL ON A RACK OR SET ON ITS SIDE, SO AIR CAN CIRCULATE AROUND IT, FOR 20 MINUTES BEFORE SLICING.

A RIFF ON THE COUNTRY BREAD:
WALNUT BREAD

EATING WALNUT BREAD WITH BUTTER AND HONEY SHOULD SEND YOU TO THAT SPECIAL PLACE IN YOUR IMAGINATION WHERE THE UNICORNS LIVE.

ONE HOUR BEFORE MIXING THE DOUGH, LIGHTLY ROAST THE WALNUTS.

PREHEAT THE OVEN TO 350°F / 180°C.

MEASURE 115 GRAMS WALNUT PIECES AND SPREAD THEM EVENLY ACROSS A BAKING SHEET OR OVENPROOF SKILLET.

ROAST FOR 6 OR 7 MINUTES, MAKING SURE NOT TO TAKE THEM TOO DARK.

LET COOL AT ROOM TEMPERATURE.

AFTER THE FLOUR, WATER, AND LEVAIN ARE MIXED IN THE AUTOLYSE STEP, ADD THE COOLED ROASTED WALNUTS ALONG WITH THE SALT.

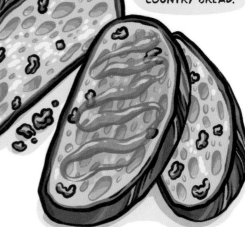

MIX THE DOUGH BY HAND, AND ALL THE REMAINING STEPS ARE THE SAME AS THE COUNTRY BREAD.

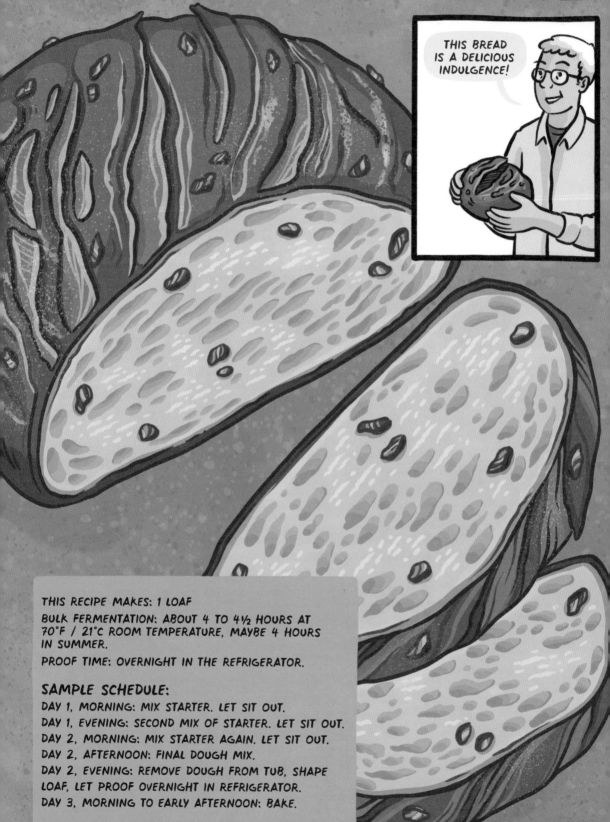

THIS RECIPE MAKES: 1 LOAF

BULK FERMENTATION: ABOUT 4 TO 4½ HOURS AT 70°F / 21°C ROOM TEMPERATURE, MAYBE 4 HOURS IN SUMMER.

PROOF TIME: OVERNIGHT IN THE REFRIGERATOR.

SAMPLE SCHEDULE:

DAY 1, MORNING: MIX STARTER. LET SIT OUT.

DAY 1, EVENING: SECOND MIX OF STARTER. LET SIT OUT.

DAY 2, MORNING: MIX STARTER AGAIN. LET SIT OUT.

DAY 2, AFTERNOON: FINAL DOUGH MIX.

DAY 2, EVENING: REMOVE DOUGH FROM TUB, SHAPE LOAF, LET PROOF OVERNIGHT IN REFRIGERATOR.

DAY 3, MORNING TO EARLY AFTERNOON: BAKE.

THE ACIDITY OF SOURDOUGH HERE REALLY COMPLEMENTS THE FATTINESS OF THE BACON.

THIS BREAD IS IMPRESSIVE EATEN STILL WARM FROM THE OVEN OR GRILLED.

IT SOARS WHEN TOASTED AND SERVED WITH EGGS AND CHILLED CIDER OR A GLASS OF BUBBLY.

IT SINGS IN A BLT SANDWICH WITH LEMONY MAYONNAISE AND FRESH RIPE TOMATOES.

IT SHINES WHEN MADE INTO WARM, CRISP CROUTONS FOR USE IN A SALAD WITH A VINAIGRETTE.

MAYBE THE ULTIMATE ELVIS SANDWICH WOULD BE THIS BACON BREAD WITH PEANUT BUTTER AND BANANAS. AND MORE BACON.

THIS DOUGH SHOULD HAVE A SLIGHTLY SHORTER FIRST RISE TIME THAN THE COUNTRY BREAD.

THE BACON FAT MAKES THE YEAST EXTRA HAPPY, SO THE DOUGH WILL DEVELOP MORE QUICKLY.

STARTER: DAY 1, MORNING

INGREDIENT	QUANTITY		
LEVAIN	50 TO 60G	¼ CUP	
WHITE FLOUR	100G	½ CUP + 3 TBSP + 1¼ TSP	
WATER	100G 75° TO 80°F / 24° TO 27°C IN SUMMER; 85°F / 29°C IN WINTER	¼ CUP + 2 TBSP + 2 TSP	

STARTER: DAY 1, EVENING

INGREDIENT	QUANTITY		
MORNING STARTER MIX	ALL OF IT		
WHITE FLOUR	100G	½ CUP + 3 TBSP + 1¼ TSP	
WATER	100G 70°F / 21°C IN SUMMER; 85°F / 29°C IN WINTER	¼ CUP + 2 TBSP + 2 TSP	

STARTER: DAY 2, MORNING

INGREDIENT	QUANTITY		
STARTER	50 TO 60G IN SUMMER; 75G IN WINTER	¼ CUP IN SUMMER; ¼ CUP + 2 TBSP IN WINTER	
WHITE FLOUR	100G	½ CUP + 3 TBSP + 1¼ TSP	
WATER	100G 90° TO 95°F / 32° TO 35°C	¼ CUP + 2 TBSP + 2 TSP	

FINAL DOUGH: DAY 2, AFTERNOON

INGREDIENT	QUANTITY		BAKER'S %
WHITE FLOUR	300G	2 CUPS + 1 TBSP + 2½ TSP	80%
WHOLE-WHEAT FLOUR	100G	½ CUP + 1 TBSP + ½ TSP	20%
WATER	300G 90° TO 95°F / 32° TO 35°C	1¼ CUPS	80%
FINE SEA SALT	11G	2¼ TSP	2.2%
STARTER	200G	1 CUP	20%
BACON	1/2 POUND UNCOOKED	CUT INTO 1-INCH PIECES WITH 1 TBSP BACON FAT RESERVED	

WEIGH AN EMPTY 2-QUART CONTAINER OR BIG BOWL.

MARK ITS WEIGHT ON THE CONTAINER'S SIDE OR WRITE IT DOWN. YOU WILL NEED THIS INFO LATER.

MEASURE 100 GRAMS (75° TO 80°F / 24° TO 27°C IN SUMMER; 85°F / 29°C IN WINTER) WATER INTO YOUR CONTAINER.

ADD 50 TO 60 GRAMS LEVAIN FROM THE REFRIGERATOR AND STIR A BIT WITH YOUR FINGERS TO LOOSEN UP THE CULTURE.

ADD 100 GRAMS WHITE BREAD FLOUR AND MIX WITH YOUR FINGERS UNTIL ALL IS INCORPORATED.

COVER WITH A LID OR PLASTIC WRAP, AND LEAVE IT OUT AT ROOM TEMPERATURE.

THIS WORKS WELL AT 70°F / 21°C ROOM TEMPERATURE.

IF YOUR KITCHEN IS MUCH WARMER THAN THAT, SAY, 75° TO 80°F / 24°C TO 27°C, USE COOLER WATER AT 65° TO 70°F / 18° TO 21°C.

PUT THE REST OF YOUR LEVAIN BACK INTO THE FRIDGE.

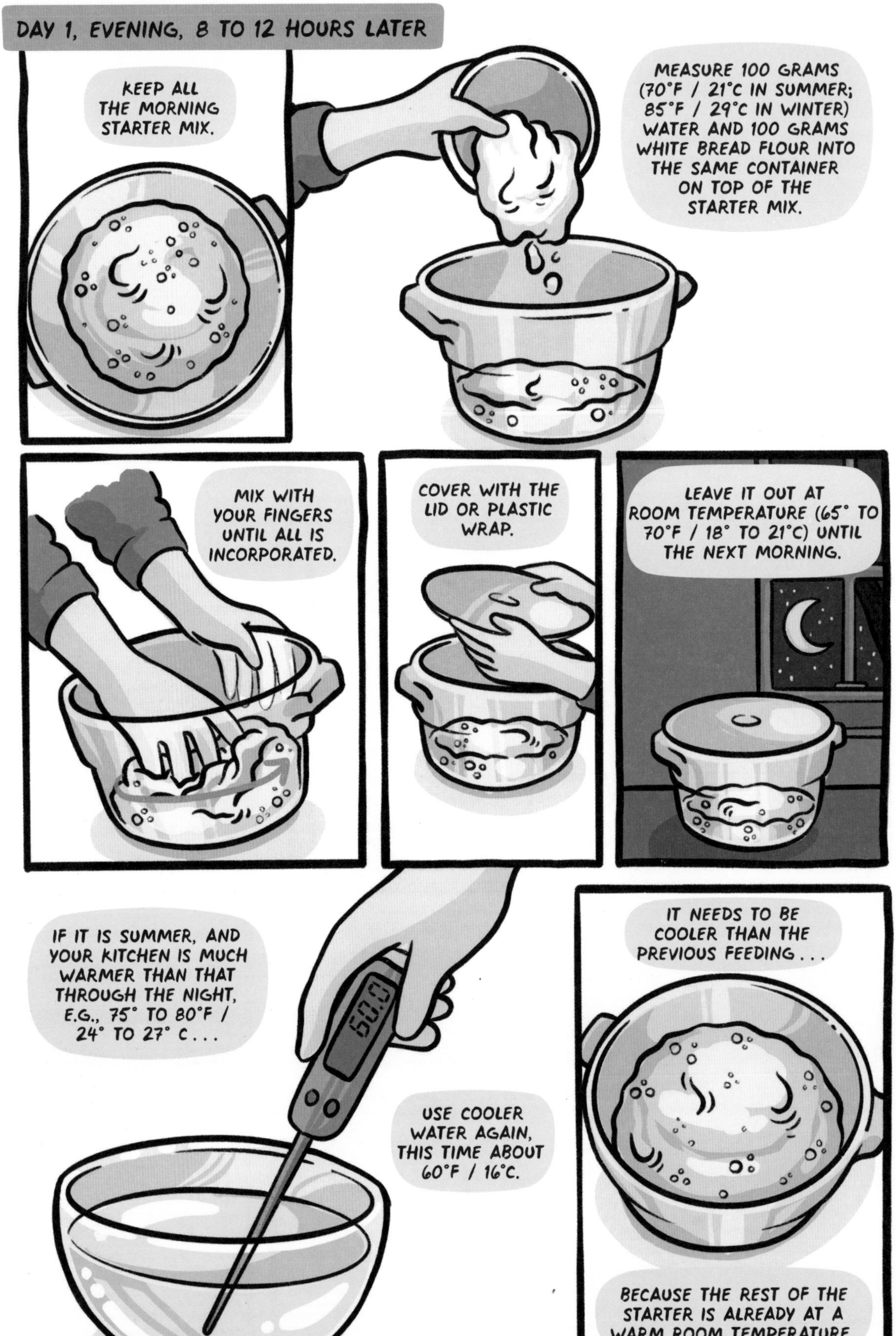
DAY 1, EVENING, 8 TO 12 HOURS LATER
KEEP ALL THE MORNING STARTER MIX.
MEASURE 100 GRAMS (70°F / 21°C IN SUMMER; 85°F / 29°C IN WINTER) WATER AND 100 GRAMS WHITE BREAD FLOUR INTO THE SAME CONTAINER ON TOP OF THE STARTER MIX.
MIX WITH YOUR FINGERS UNTIL ALL IS INCORPORATED.
COVER WITH THE LID OR PLASTIC WRAP.
LEAVE IT OUT AT ROOM TEMPERATURE (65° TO 70°F / 18° TO 21°C) UNTIL THE NEXT MORNING.
IF IT IS SUMMER, AND YOUR KITCHEN IS MUCH WARMER THAN THAT THROUGH THE NIGHT, E.G., 75° TO 80°F / 24° TO 27° C . . .
60.0
USE COOLER WATER AGAIN, THIS TIME ABOUT 60°F / 16°C.
IT NEEDS TO BE COOLER THAN THE PREVIOUS FEEDING . . .
BECAUSE THE REST OF THE STARTER IS ALREADY AT A WARM ROOM TEMPERATURE.

AROUND 8 A.M., REFERENCE THE EMPTY CONTAINER WEIGHT AND REMOVE ALL BUT 50 TO 60 GRAMS (75 GRAMS IN THE WINTER) OF THE DAY 1 STARTER FROM YOUR CONTAINER.

YOU CAN TOSS THE REST, OR USE IT TO MAKE THE EXCELLENT PIZZA DOUGHS ON PAGES 143 AND 146.

MEASURE 100 GRAMS (95°F / 35°C) WATER INTO THE CONTAINER WITH THE STARTER AND MIX WITH YOUR FINGERS UNTIL YOU HAVE A SLURRY.

ADD 100 GRAMS WHITE BREAD FLOUR. MIX WITH YOUR FINGERS UNTIL ALL IS INCORPORATED.

KEEP IN A WARM PLACE, 70° TO 75°F / 21° TO 24°C.

DAY 2, AFTERNOON, 7 TO 8 HOURS LATER — 1A. COOK THE BACON

WITH A SHARP KNIFE, SLICE THE BACON STRIPS INTO 1-INCH WIDTHS.

COOK THE BACON IN A LARGE SKILLET OVER MEDIUM HEAT UNTIL CRISP.

DRAIN ON PAPER TOWELS . . .

AND RESERVE 1 TABLESPOON OF THE RENDERED BACON FAT FOR THE DOUGH.

LET THE BACON COOL, AND THEN CRUMBLE.

1B: AUTOLYSE

MEASURE 300 GRAMS (90° TO 95°F / 32° TO 35°C) WATER INTO A 6-QUART ROUND TUB OR SIMILAR CONTAINER.

WET YOUR HAND AND ADD 200 GRAMS OF THE DAY 2 STARTER YOU MIXED IN THE MORNING.

STIR A BIT WITH YOUR FINGERS TO LOOSEN UP THE CULTURE.

ADD 300 GRAMS WHITE BREAD FLOUR, AND 100 GRAMS WHOLE-WHEAT FLOUR.

MIX IT BY HAND UNTIL ALL IS INCORPORATED.

SPRINKLE 11 GRAMS FINE SEA SALT AND ALL OF THE BACON EVENLY ACROSS THE TOP OF THE AUTOLYSE DOUGH.

COVER AND LET REST FOR 20 MINUTES.

WET YOUR WORKING HAND BEFORE MIXING SO THE DOUGH DOESN'T STICK TO YOU.

REACH UNDERNEATH THE DOUGH AND GRAB ABOUT ONE-FOURTH OF IT.

GENTLY STRETCH THIS SECTION AND FOLD IT OVER THE TOP TO THE OTHER SIDE OF THE DOUGH.

REPEAT 3 MORE TIMES WITH THE REMAINING DOUGH UNTIL THE SALT AND BACON ARE FULLY ENCLOSED.

MAKE 5 OR 6 PINCER CUTS ACROSS THE ENTIRE MASS OF DOUGH.

THEN FOLD THE DOUGH OVER ITSELF A FEW TIMES.

REPEAT, ALTERNATELY CUTTING AND FOLDING, UNTIL ALL THE BACON PIECES ARE FULLY INTEGRATED.

COVER AND LET THE DOUGH REST FOR A FEW MINUTES . . .

THEN FOLD FOR ANOTHER 30 SECONDS OR UNTIL THE DOUGH TIGHTENS UP.

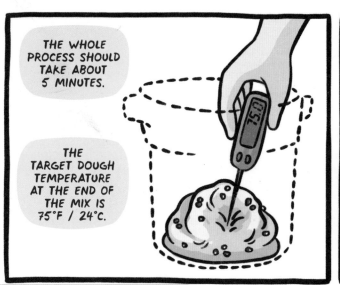

THE WHOLE PROCESS SHOULD TAKE ABOUT 5 MINUTES.

THE TARGET DOUGH TEMPERATURE AT THE END OF THE MIX IS 75°F / 24°C.

COVER THE TUB AND LET THE DOUGH REST FOR 10 MINUTES.

2B: MIX IN THE BACON FAT

SPREAD THE 1 TABLESPOON OF BACON FAT OVER THE TOP OF THE DOUGH.

INCORPORATE IT INTO THE DOUGH, AGAIN USING THE PINCER METHOD, ALTERNATING WITH FOLDING, UNTIL THE BACON FAT IS EVENLY DISTRIBUTED.

COVER THE TUB AND LET THE DOUGH RISE UNTIL THE NEXT FOLD.

3: FOLD & FIRST RISE

THIS DOUGH NEEDS 3 FOLDS.

IT'S EASIEST TO APPLY THE FOLDS DURING THE FIRST 1½ HOURS AFTER MIXING THE DOUGH.

APPLY THE FIRST FOLD ABOUT 10 MINUTES AFTER MIXING . . .

AND THE SECOND AND THIRD WHEN YOU SEE THE DOUGH SPREAD OUT IN THE TUB FROM THE PREVIOUS FOLD.

IF NEED BE, IT'S OK TO FOLD LATER; JUST BE SURE TO LEAVE IT ALONE FOR THE LAST HOUR OF RISING.

WHEN THE DOUGH IS ABOUT 2½ TIMES ITS ORIGINAL VOLUME, AND THE EDGE OF THE DOUGH IS ABOUT ½ INCH BELOW THE 2-QUART LINE IN THE DOUGH TUB . . .

IT'S READY TO BE MADE UP INTO A LOAF.

IF IT IS IN A ROOM AT 70°F / 21°C, THIS FIRST FERMENT SHOULD TAKE 4 TO 4½ HOURS.

THIS DOUGH RISES A LITTLE FASTER THAN THE COUNTRY BREAD BECAUSE THE BACON FAT ADDS EXTRA FOOD FOR THE YEAST. YUM!

JUDGE WHEN ITS READY BASED ON VOLUME EXPANSION MORE THAN TIME.

IF YOUR KITCHEN IS WARMER OR COLDER THAN MINE, YOUR TIME WILL VARY.

IF YOU'RE NOT USING A MARKED DOUGH TUB, YOU'LL HAVE TO EYEBALL IT. USE YOUR BEST JUDGMENT.

DAY 2, EVENING — 4: REMOVE THE DOUGH FROM ITS TUB

LIGHTLY FLOUR A WORK SURFACE ABOUT 12 INCHES WIDE.

FLOUR YOUR HANDS.

SPRINKLE A BIT OF FLOUR AROUND THE EDGES OF THE TUB.

TIP THE TUB SLIGHTLY, AND GENTLY WORK YOUR FLOURED FREE HAND BENEATH THE DOUGH TO LOOSEN IT FROM THE BOTTOM OF THE TUB.

THEN TURN THE TUB ON ITS SIDE AND EASE THE DOUGH OUT ONTO THE WORK SURFACE WITHOUT PULLING OR TEARING IT.

5: SHAPE

DUST A PROOFING BASKET MODERATELY WITH FLOUR AND SPREAD THE FLOUR AROUND WITH YOUR HAND.

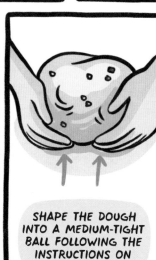

SHAPE THE DOUGH INTO A MEDIUM-TIGHT BALL FOLLOWING THE INSTRUCTIONS ON PAGE 34.

PLACE IT SEAM SIDE DOWN IN ITS PROOFING BASKET.

6: PROOF

PLACE THE BASKET IN A PLASTIC BAG, AND TUCK THE BAG UNDER THE BASKET.

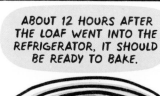

REFRIGERATE OVERNIGHT.

ABOUT 12 HOURS AFTER THE LOAF WENT INTO THE REFRIGERATOR, IT SHOULD BE READY TO BAKE.

IT DOES NOT NEED TO COME TO ROOM TEMPERATURE FIRST.

ABOUT 45 MINUTES PRIOR TO BAKING, POSITION A RACK IN THE MIDDLE OF THE OVEN . . .

AND PUT A DUTCH OVEN, WITH ITS LID, ON THE RACK.

PREHEAT THE OVEN TO 475°F / 245°C.

8: BAKE

INVERT THE BASKET WITH ITS PROOFED LOAF ONTO A LIGHTLY FLOURED COUNTERTOP.

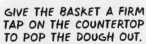

GIVE THE BASKET A FIRM TAP ON THE COUNTERTOP TO POP THE DOUGH OUT.

THE TOP OF THE LOAF WILL BE THE SIDE THAT WAS FACING DOWN WHILE IT WAS RISING – THE SEAM SIDE.

FOR THE NEXT STEP, PLEASE BE CAREFUL NOT TO LET YOUR HANDS, FINGERS, OR FOREARMS TOUCH THE EXTREMELY HOT DUTCH OVEN.

USE OVEN MITTS TO REMOVE THE PREHEATED DUTCH OVEN FROM YOUR OVEN.

REMOVE THE LID AND CAREFULLY PLACE THE LOAF SEAM SIDE UP IN THE HOT DUTCH OVEN.

USE THE MITTS TO REPLACE THE LID.

RETURN THE DUTCH OVEN TO THE CENTER OF THE MIDDLE RACK, AND BAKE FOR 30 MINUTES.

THEN CAREFULLY REMOVE THE LID AND BAKE FOR ABOUT 20 MINUTES MORE, UNTIL DARK BROWN ALL AROUND THE LOAF.

CHECK AFTER 15 MINUTES OF BAKING UNCOVERED IN CASE YOUR OVEN RUNS HOT.

REMOVE THE DUTCH OVEN AND CAREFULLY TILT IT TO TURN THE LOAF OUT.

LET THE LOAF COOL ON A RACK OR SET ON ITS SIDE, SO AIR CAN CIRCULATE AROUND IT, FOR 20 MINUTES BEFORE SLICING.

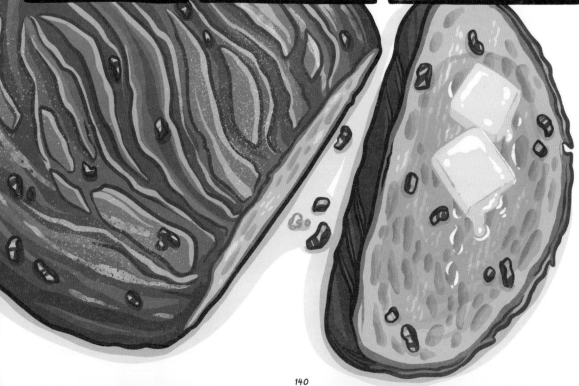

"EXTRA" LEVAIN STARTER

WHEN YOU'RE ONLY MAKING ONE OR TWO LOAVES OF SOURDOUGH, YOU'RE BOUND TO MAKE MORE LEVAIN CULTURE THAN YOU NEED.

IT COMES FROM THE NEED TO CREATE ENOUGH LEAVENING POWER IN THE CULTURE AND TO BUILD A BALANCE OF GOOD FLAVORS.

FOR THIS BOOK'S DUTCH OVEN LEVAIN BREADS, I HAVE YOU MAKE UP A STARTER FROM A REFRIGERATED LEVAIN.

THE FINAL STARTER FEEDING ON DAY 2 HAS YOU REMOVE ABOUT 400 GRAMS OF STARTER . . .

LEAVING BEHIND 50 TO 60 GRAMS FOR THE BUILDUP FOR THE FINAL DOUGH MIX.

THERE ARE MANY OPTIONS FOR MAKING SOMETHING ELSE FROM THE EXTRA STARTER!

PIZZA DOUGH IS MY FAVORITE CHOICE.

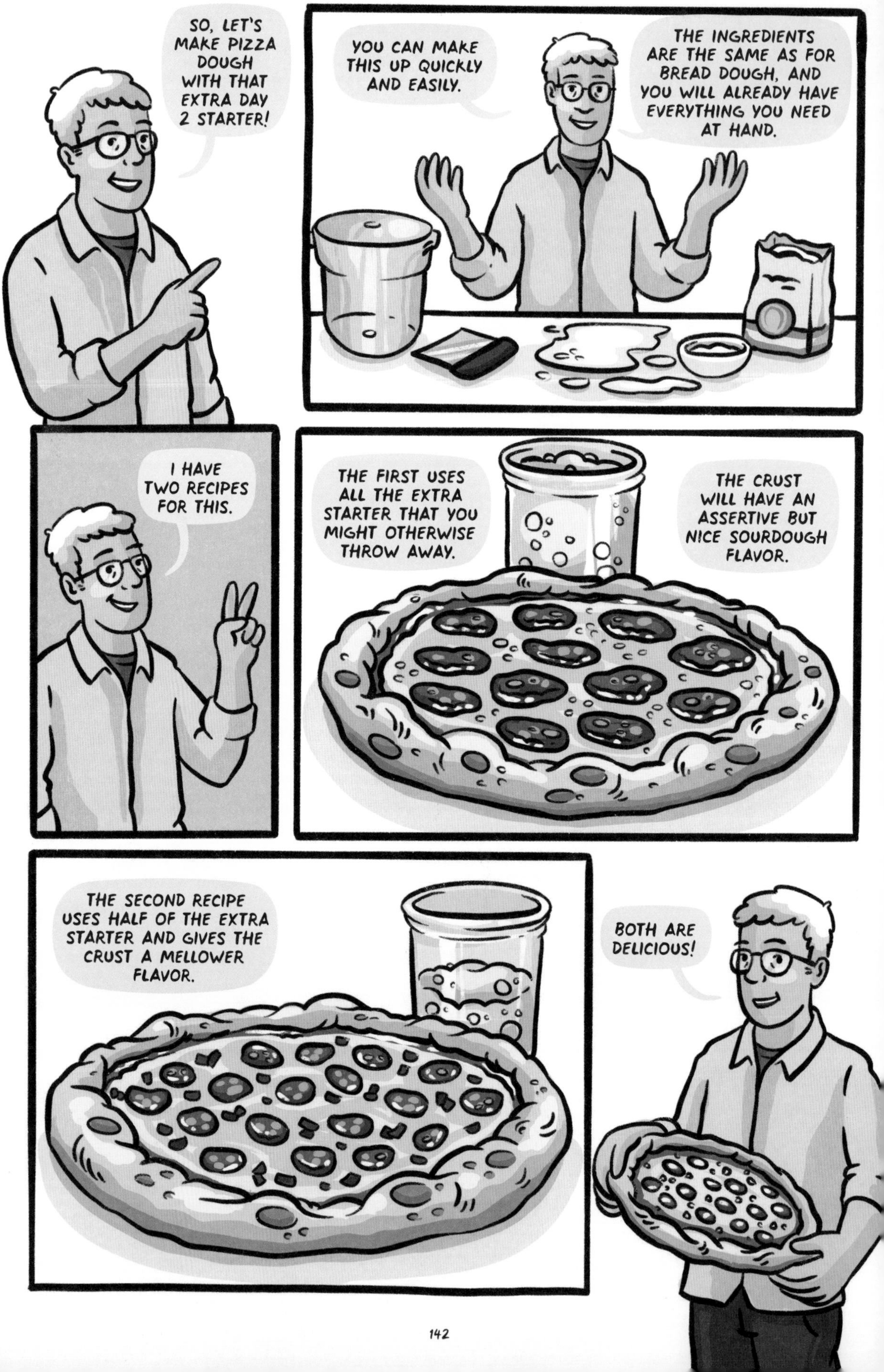

SO, LET'S MAKE PIZZA DOUGH WITH THAT EXTRA DAY 2 STARTER!
YOU CAN MAKE THIS UP QUICKLY AND EASILY.
THE INGREDIENTS ARE THE SAME AS FOR BREAD DOUGH, AND YOU WILL ALREADY HAVE EVERYTHING YOU NEED AT HAND.
I HAVE TWO RECIPES FOR THIS.
THE FIRST USES ALL THE EXTRA STARTER THAT YOU MIGHT OTHERWISE THROW AWAY.
THE CRUST WILL HAVE AN ASSERTIVE BUT NICE SOURDOUGH FLAVOR.
THE SECOND RECIPE USES HALF OF THE EXTRA STARTER AND GIVES THE CRUST A MELLOWER FLAVOR.
BOTH ARE DELICIOUS!

FRUITY, FULL-FLAVOR SOURDOUGH
PIZZA DOUGH
WITH ALL of the EXTRA STARTER

THIS RECIPE MAKES 823 GRAMS OF PIZZA DOUGH, ENOUGH FOR 3 12-INCH PIZZAS OR 1 PAN PIZZA.

FIRST RISE: 1 HOUR

PROOF TIME: 4 TO 5 HOURS AT 70°F / 21°C, OR REFRIGERATE AFTER 3 HOURS TO MAKE PIZZA WITHIN THE NEXT 3 DAYS.

INGREDIENT	QUANTITY		BAKER'S %
BREAD FLOUR OR PIZZA FLOUR*	300G	2 CUPS + 2 TBSP + 1¼ TSP	100%
WATER	140G 80°F / 27°C	½ CUP + 2 TBSP	67%**
FINE SEA SALT	13G	2½ TSP	2.7%
STARTER	370G	1¾ CUP + 1 TBSP	38%

* TOTAL FLOUR INCLUDING FLOUR IN STARTER = 485 GRAMS
** INCLUDES WATER IN STARTER

1: MIX THE DOUGH

MEASURE 140 GRAMS (80°F / 27°C) WATER IN A 6-QUART ROUND TUB OR SIMILAR CONTAINER.

ADD 13G SALT AND STIR IT AROUND WITH YOUR HAND UNTIL IT DISSOLVES.

ADD 370 GRAMS STARTER (APPROXIMATE AMOUNTS ARE FINE), AND MIX WITH THE WATER BY HAND.

MIX IN THE FLOUR IN TWO STAGES.

FIRST, ADD 200 GRAMS OF THE FLOUR AND MIX BY HAND UNTIL A DOUGH IS FORMED.

THEN ADD THE OTHER 100 GRAMS FLOUR AND COMPLETE THE MIX BY HAND, USING THE SAME PINCER METHOD AS FOR BREAD DOUGH.

THIS PIZZA DOUGH IS STIFFER THAN MY BREAD DOUGHS, AND IT'S EASIER TO DO THIS 2-STAGE METHOD WHEN MIXING BY HAND.

COVER AND LET REST FOR 10 MINUTES.

THEN FOLD THE DOUGH OVER ITSELF A FEW TIMES UNTIL YOU GET A ROUND OF DOUGH.

COVER AND LET REST FOR 1 HOUR.

2: DIVIDE AND MAKE UP DOUGH BALLS

DIVIDE THE DOUGH INTO 3 EQUAL PORTIONS ABOUT 275 GRAMS EACH.

SHAPE EACH INTO A ROUND BALL.

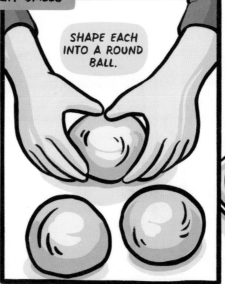

WRAP EACH DOUGH BALL IN PLASTIC WRAP, LEAVING AN EXTRA ½ INCH AROUND THE SIDES FOR EXPANSION.

AND THEN MAKE PIZZA!

LET THE DOUGH BALLS SIT OUT FOR 4 TO 5 HOURS AT ROOM TEMPERATURE . . .

OR, MY FAVORITE, REFRIGERATE THE DOUGH BALLS AFTER 4 TO 5 HOURS FOR 1 TO 3 DAYS.

THE TEXTURE OF THE CRUST WILL BE MORE DELICATE.

IF YOU REFRIGERATE, MAKE SURE TO LET THE DOUGH WARM UP AND RELAX ENOUGH SO IT STRETCHES OUT EASILY.

MELLOWER SOURDOUGH
PIZZA DOUGH
WITH HALF OF THE EXTRA STARTER

THIS RECIPE MAKES 848 GRAMS OF
PIZZA DOUGH, ENOUGH FOR 3 12-INCH
PIZZAS OR 1 PAN PIZZA.

FIRST RISE: 1 HOUR

PROOF TIME: 4 TO 5 HOURS AT 70°F / 21°C,
OR REFRIGERATE AFTER 3 HOURS TO MAKE
PIZZA WITHIN THE NEXT 3 DAYS.

INGREDIENT	QUANTITY		BAKER'S %
BREAD FLOUR OR PIZZA FLOUR*	400G	2 ¾ CUPS + 2 TSP	100%
WATER	235G 80°F / 27°C	½ CUP + 2 TBSP	67%**
FINE SEA SALT	13G	2 ½ TSP	2.6%
STARTER	200G	1 CUP	20%

* TOTAL FLOUR INCLUDING FLOUR IN STARTER = 485 GRAMS
** INCLUDES WATER IN STARTER

1: MIX THE DOUGH

MEASURE 235 GRAMS
(80°F / 27°C) WATER IN A
6-QUART ROUND TUB OR
SIMILAR CONTAINER.

ADD 13G SALT AND
STIR IT AROUND WITH
YOUR HAND UNTIL IT
DISSOLVES.

ADD 200 GRAMS
STARTER
(APPROXIMATE
AMOUNTS ARE FINE),
AND MIX WITH THE
WATER BY HAND.

MIX IN THE FLOUR IN TWO STAGES.

THIS PIZZA DOUGH IS STIFFER THAN MY BREAD DOUGHS, AND IT'S EASIER TO DO THIS 2-STAGE METHOD WHEN MIXING BY HAND.

FIRST, ADD 300 GRAMS OF THE FLOUR AND MIX BY HAND UNTIL A DOUGH IS FORMED.

THEN ADD THE OTHER 100 GRAMS FLOUR AND COMPLETE THE MIX BY HAND, USING THE SAME PINCER METHOD AS FOR BREAD DOUGH.

COVER AND LET REST FOR 10 MINUTES.

THEN FOLD THE DOUGH OVER ITSELF A FEW TIMES UNTIL YOU GET A ROUND OF DOUGH.

COVER AND LET REST FOR 1 HOUR.

2: DIVIDE AND MAKE UP DOUGH BALLS

DIVIDE THE DOUGH INTO 3 EQUAL PORTIONS ABOUT 280 GRAMS EACH.

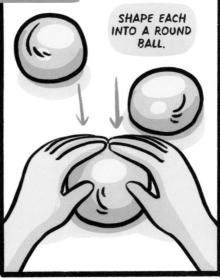

SHAPE EACH INTO A ROUND BALL.

WRAP EACH DOUGH BALL IN PLASTIC WRAP, LEAVING AN EXTRA ½ INCH AROUND THE SIDES FOR EXPANSION.

3: DOUGH BALL RISE

LET THE DOUGH BALLS SIT OUT FOR 4 TO 5 HOURS AT ROOM TEMPERATURE . . .

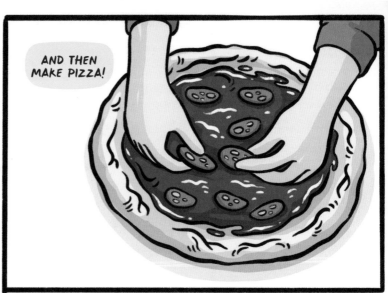

AND THEN MAKE PIZZA!

OR, MY FAVORITE, REFRIGERATE THE DOUGH BALLS AFTER 4 TO 5 HOURS FOR 1 TO 3 DAYS.

THE TEXTURE OF THE CRUST WILL BE MORE DELICATE.

IF YOU REFRIGERATE, MAKE SURE TO LET THE DOUGH WARM UP AND RELAX ENOUGH SO IT STRETCHES OUT EASILY.

PIZZA SAUCE

BUY A 28-OUNCE CAN OF BEST-QUALITY WHOLE PEELED TOMATOES.

THE SAUCE IS ONLY AS GOOD AS THE TOMATOES.

COMBINE ALL THE TOMATOES WITH 8 GRAMS (1½ TEASPOONS) SEA SALT IN A BLENDER, AND BLEND FOR JUST 2 SECONDS.

IT'S DONE! A LITTLE CHUNKY IS FINE.

OVERMIXING THE SAUCE MAKES IT TOO WATERY.

PIZZA-MAKING TIPS

MAKE SURE YOUR DOUGH BALL IS FULLY RELAXED SO IT STRETCHES OUT EASILY. IF THE DOUGH BALL IS TIGHT, IT NEEDS MORE TIME.

⅓ CUP (ABOUT 80 GRAMS) IS THE IDEAL AMOUNT OF PIZZA SAUCE FOR A 12-INCH PIZZA.

BE PREPARED TO PUT YOUR PIZZA IN THE OVEN AS SOON AS YOU FINISH TOPPING IT.

TOO LONG AFTER, AND THE PIZZA MIGHT STICK TO YOUR PEEL.

THE FINAL PROOF

BAKING YOUR OWN DELICIOUS, INCREDIBLE BREAD AT HOME IS A REWARDING EXPERIENCE!

REALLY DIGGING YOUR HANDS IN THE DOUGH IS SUCH A SATISFYING TACTILE SENSATION.

AND LEARNING THE RHYTHMS AND PATTERNS OF A DOUGH RISE CAN BE FASCINATING AND FUN.

BAKING PROFESSIONAL-QUALITY BREAD DOESN'T NEED TO BE INTIMIDATING!

THESE RECIPES MAY TAKE AWHILE TO FULLY RISE AND PROOF . . .

BUT THEY WON'T TAKE A LOT OF ACTIVE TIME OUT OF YOUR SCHEDULE.

. . .

REMEMBER THAT TIME AND TEMPERATURE ARE IMPORTANT INGREDIENTS.

BE AWARE OF THE TEMPERATURE OF YOUR WATER, AND ALSO THE AMBIENT TEMPERATURE OF YOUR KITCHEN.

AND DON'T FORGET TO MAKE ADJUSTMENTS FOR THE SEASONS!

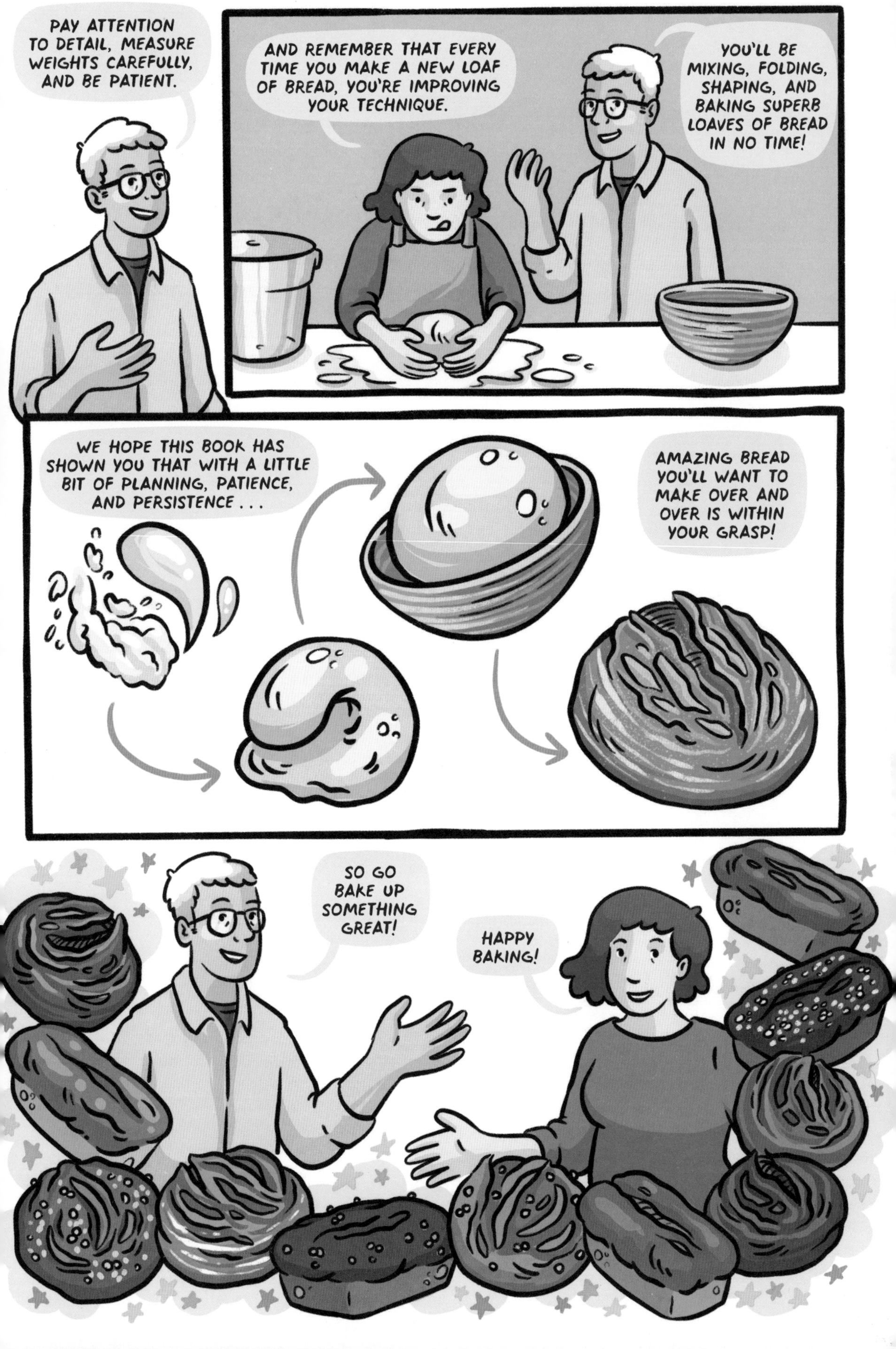
PAY ATTENTION TO DETAIL, MEASURE WEIGHTS CAREFULLY, AND BE PATIENT.
AND REMEMBER THAT EVERY TIME YOU MAKE A NEW LOAF OF BREAD, YOU'RE IMPROVING YOUR TECHNIQUE.
YOU'LL BE MIXING, FOLDING, SHAPING, AND BAKING SUPERB LOAVES OF BREAD IN NO TIME!
WE HOPE THIS BOOK HAS SHOWN YOU THAT WITH A LITTLE BIT OF PLANNING, PATIENCE, AND PERSISTENCE . . .
AMAZING BREAD YOU'LL WANT TO MAKE OVER AND OVER IS WITHIN YOUR GRASP!
SO GO BAKE UP SOMETHING GREAT!
HAPPY BAKING!

SPECIAL THANKS TO:

KIMMY TEJASINDHU

CHLOE RAWLINS

AMY COLLINS

KELLY SNOWDEN

ISABELLE GIOFFREDI

LIZ WAYNE AND DENISE BREWER

BLANCA AND STEVE HURLEY

MARK BARANOWSKI
AND EILEEN DAILEY

BECKIE GAUTREAU

NILES BARANOWSKI

TOKI WARTOOTH
BECAN-BARANOWSKI

LIZ ANNA KOZIK

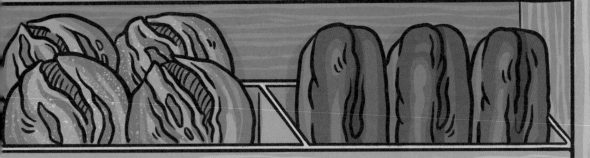

JUNIOR

LEFTY, CASEY, BROOKS, AND GOMEZ

CORINNE MUCHA

LAURA PARK

GREGG AND TONYA
TOMLINSON

KATELYN SEGER

MATEO AND THE STAFF
OF SIPPING TURTLE CAFE

KEN FORKISH

KEN FORKISH IS THE FOUNDER OF KEN'S ARTISAN BAKERY, KEN'S ARTISAN PIZZA, AND CHECKERBOARD PIZZA, ALL IN PORTLAND, OREGON. HE IS ALSO THE AUTHOR OF THE JAMES BEARD AWARD— AND IACP AWARD—WINNING BOOK *FLOUR WATER SALT YEAST*; A 2016 ODE TO PIZZA, *THE ELEMENTS OF PIZZA*; AND THE 2022 BOOK *EVOLUTIONS IN BREAD*.

KEN WAS A KEY CONTRIBUTOR TO PORTLAND'S CULINARY EVOLUTION, FOUNDING KEN'S ARTISAN BAKERY IN 2001 AND KEN'S ARTISAN PIZZA IN 2006. HE WAS A FINALIST FOR THE NATIONAL JAMES BEARD AWARD FOR OUTSTANDING PASTRY CHEF IN 2013 AND OUTSTANDING BAKER IN 2017. IN 2013, KEN OPENED TRIFECTA TAVERN & BAKERY, AN AWARD-WINNING BAR, RESTAURANT, AND SMALL-BATCH BAKERY THAT CLOSED AT ITS PEAK IN LATE 2019. KEN'S ARTISAN BAKERY WAS SOLD TO TWO LONG-STANDING EMPLOYEES, AND KEN'S ARTISAN PIZZA WAS SOLD TO A LONGTIME FRIEND.

KEN NOW LIVES IN HAWAII WITH HIS RECIPE TESTER, JUNIOR.

SARAH BECAN

SARAH BECAN HAS BEEN DRAWING COMICS SINCE SHE WAS VERY SMALL.

SHE CREATED THE WEBCOMIC "I THINK YOU'RE SAUCEOME" IN 2010, GOING ON TO PUBLISH WORK IN SAVEUR MAGAZINE, EATER, CHICAGO READER, AND TASTING TABLE, AMONG OTHERS.

SHE WAS AWARDED A XERIC GRANT AND A STUMPTOWN TROPHY FOR OUTSTANDING DEBUT FOR HER FIRST GRAPHIC NOVEL, THE COMPLETE OUIJA INTERVIEWS, AND RELEASED HER SECOND GRAPHIC NOVEL, SHUTEYE, IN 2012.

SARAH ILLUSTRATED THE COOKBOOK THE ADVENTURES OF FAT RICE, PUBLISHED IN 2016, AND IS THE COAUTHOR AND ILLUSTRATOR OF LET'S MAKE RAMEN!, PUBLISHED IN JULY 2019, AND LET'S MAKE DUMPLINGS!, PUBLISHED IN JUNE 2021.

SHE LIVES IN CHICAGO WITH HER PARTNER, NILES, AND THEIR CAT, TOKI, AND IF SHE HAD IT HER WAY, SHE'D DO NOTHING BUT DRAW PICTURES OF FOOD ALL DAY.

INDEX

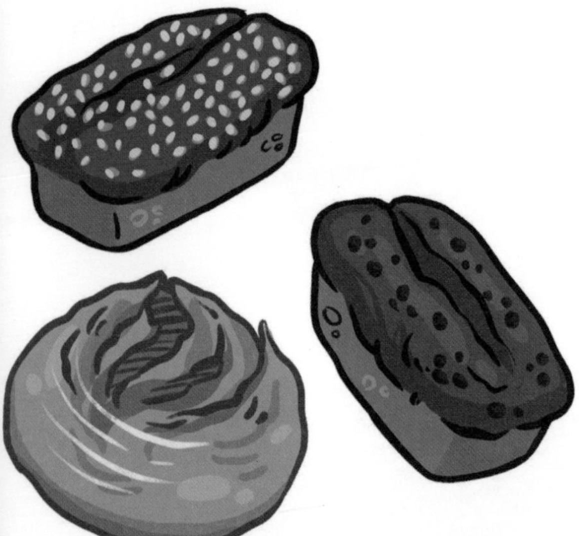

LIBRARY OF CONGRESS CATALOGING-IN-PUBLICATION DATA

NAMES: FORKISH, KEN, AUTHOR. | BECAN, SARAH, 1976- ILLUSTRATOR.
TITLE: LET'S MAKE BREAD! : A COMIC BOOK COOKBOOK / KEN FORKISH, SARAH BECAN.
DESCRIPTION: FIRST EDITION. | EMERYVILLE : TEN SPEED PRESS, 2024. | INCLUDES INDEX.
IDENTIFIERS: LCCN 2023027969 (PRINT) | LCCN 2023027970 (EBOOK)
| ISBN 9781984860873 (TRADE PAPERBACK) | ISBN 9781984860880 (EBOOK)
SUBJECTS: LCSH: COOKING (BREAD) | BREAD. | LCGFT: COOKBOOKS. | GRAPHIC NOVELS.
CLASSIFICATION: LCC TX769 .F675 2024 (PRINT) | LCC TX769 (EBOOK)
| DDC 641.81/5--DC23/ENG/20231205
LC RECORD AVAILABLE AT HTTPS://LCCN.LOC.GOV/2023027969
LC EBOOK RECORD AVAILABLE AT HTTPS://LCCN.LOC.GOV/2023027970

TRADE PAPERBACK ISBN: 978-1-9848-6087-3
EBOOK ISBN: 978-1-9848-6088-0

PRINTED IN CHINA

EDITOR: KIMMY TEJASINDHU | PRODUCTION EDITOR: TERRY DEAL
DESIGNER: ISABELLE GIOFFREDI | ART DIRECTOR: CHLOE RAWLINS
PRODUCTION MANAGER: JANE CHINN
COPYEDITOR: RACHEL MARKOWITZ
PROOFREADERS: MARK MCCAUSLIN AND TRICIA WYGAL
COMPOSITOR: HANNAH HUNT
INDEXER: KEN DELLAPENTA

1 3 5 7 9 10 8 6 4 2

FIRST EDITION

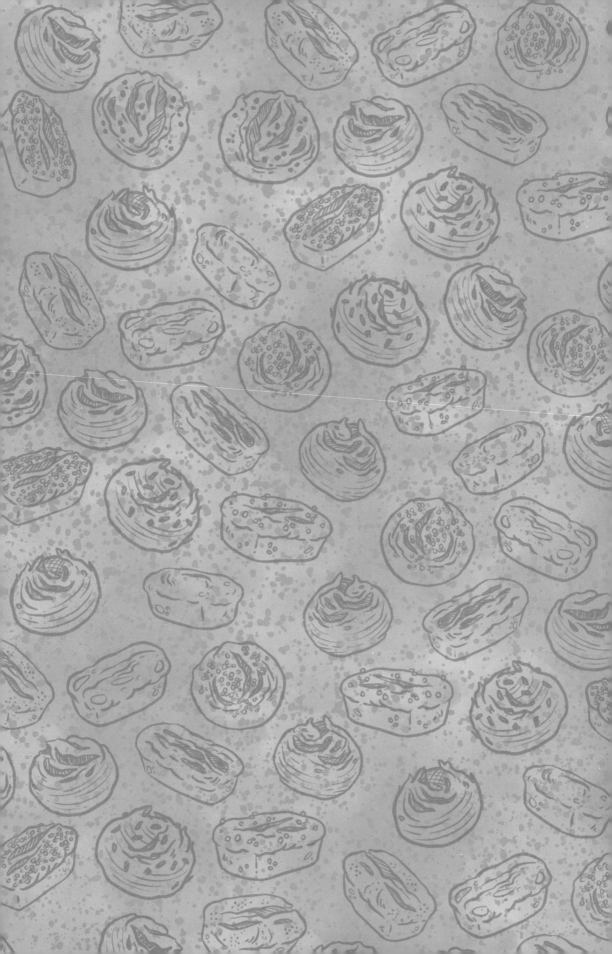

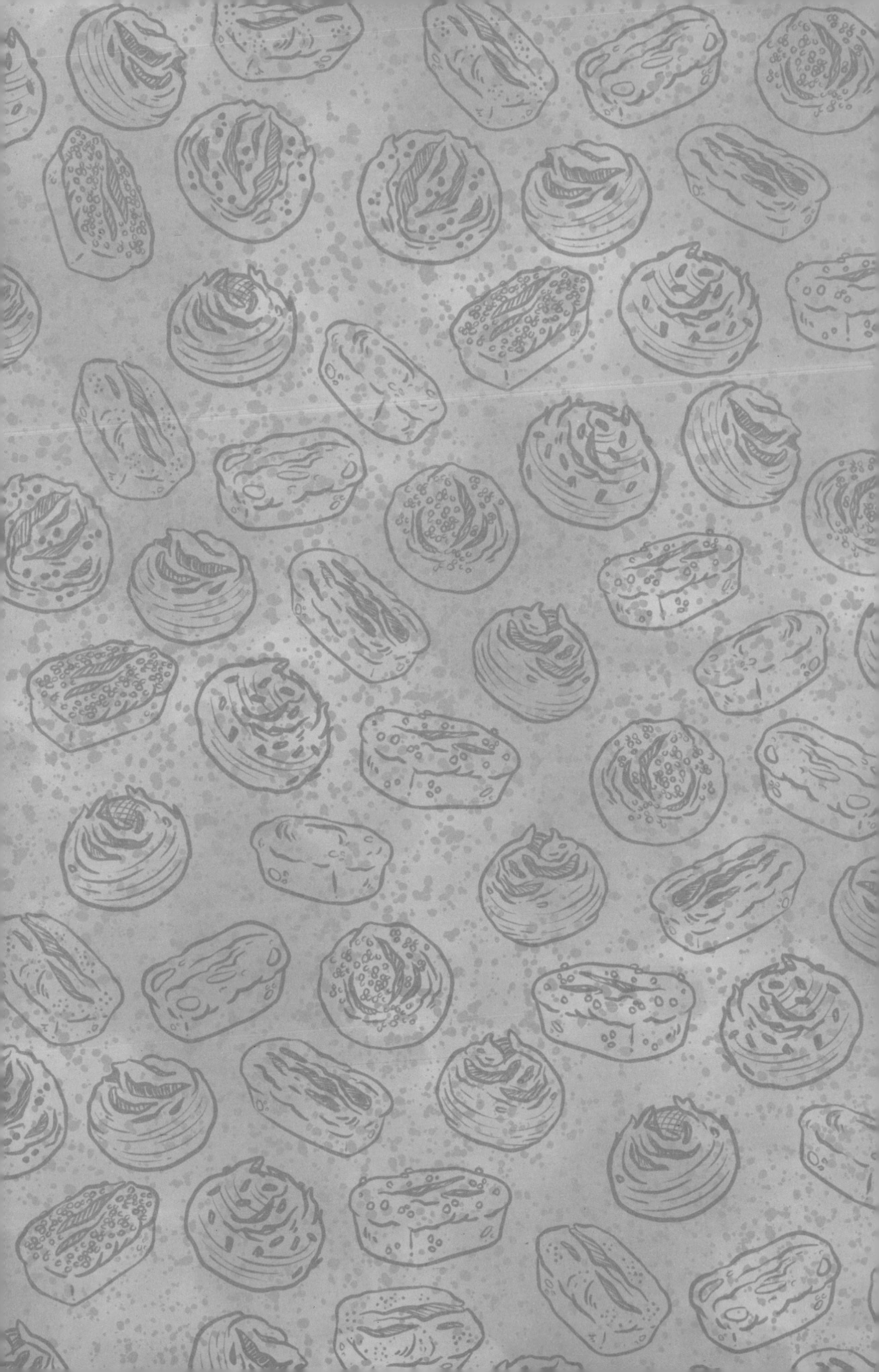